HO__
WOULD
JESUS
LEAD
WORSHIP

Sara & Sam Hargreaves

How Would Jesus Lead Worship?: Fully Revised and Updated Second Edition
Copyright © 2020 Sara and Sam Hargreaves

This Second Edition published by Music and Worship Foundation CIO
Registered office: 8a Horley Close, Bexleyheath, Kent, DA6 7HS
www.mwf.org.uk
MWF is a registered charity, number 1175280

ISBN 978-0-9935799-8-1
A catalogue record for this book is available from the British Library

First published in 2009 by the Bible Reading Fellowship, www.brf.org.uk

Unless otherwise stated, scripture quotations are taken from the *Holy Bible,* New International Version® Anglicised, NIV® Copyright © 1979, 1984, 2011 by Biblica, Inc.® Used by permission. All rights reserved worldwide.

Scripture quotations marked MSG are taken from *THE MESSAGE*, copyright © 1993, 2002, 2018 by Eugene H. Peterson. Used by permission of NavPress. All rights reserved. Represented by Tyndale House Publishers, Inc.

Scripture quotations marked NLT are taken from the *Holy Bible*, New Living Translation, copyright © 1996, 2004, 2015 by Tyndale House Foundation. Used by permission of Tyndale House Publishers, Inc., Carol Stream, Illinois 60188. All rights reserved.

Typeset by Richard Lyall - http://www.richardlyall.co.uk

engageworship is a ministry of the Music and Worship Foundation CIO. We exist to resource and train local churches for innovative, creative and world changing worship. For free downloadable resources, information on our training events or to order further books visit www. engageworship.org

CONTENTS

INTRODUCTION TO THE 2ND EDITION

The first edition of *How Would Jesus Lead Worship* came out in 2009. Since then we have been teaching this material to local churches, conferences and networks across the UK. We have continued to find the idea of Jesus as our true worship leader foundational and releasing. And each time we open the gospels, Jesus' example challenges and encourages us to be more Christ-like worship leaders.

So the heart of this book has not changed - but we have! We are ten years older, and our experiences are wider and more varied. Back then we'd only worked full-time in a busy, creative Anglican church in London. Since the book came out we've subsequently worked part-time in a rural parish, volunteered in a Baptist church as worship coordinators and then helped run a fresh expression of church in a park. Sam spent five years on the faculty at London School of Theology, and together Sara and Sam have run engageworship. This ministry has grown to a full-time pursuit: creating resources, modelling worship-leading and delivering training to a wide variety of contexts and denominations.

As a result, we've been able to approach this second edition with fresh eyes. The outline remains the same but we have fully revised the entire text, adding new stories, fresh examples, wider perspectives, and quietly editing out some of our younger selves' more embarrassing turns of phrase. It is a rare treat to be able to re-shape your previous work, and we're excited to share this 'remastered' version with you.

We're really grateful to our original editor, Naomi Starkey, and to BRF for not only supporting the first edition but also generously passing on the full rights to us so we could embark on this second edition. We are also indebted to our team of friends and Music and Worship Foundation trustees who have read and fed back on this new edition: Timo Scharnowski, Ron Jones, Eils Osgood, Andy Mitchell, Roger Peach, Eils Osgood, John Leach, Sylvia Kalisch and Damian Herbert. Thanks also to Richard Lyall for typesetting and Konni Deppe for proof reading.

Most of all we want to thank everyone who contributed so generously to the crowdfunding campaign, making possible not only this book but the free video series which accompanies it. They are:

Andrea Lowndes, Andrew and Jayne Mitchell, Angela and Jeremy Perigo, Anne Stratton, Brian Hoare, Cathie Taylor, the Chinese Church in London, Christ Church Downend, Craig Owen, Di Oliver, Dominic Eaton, Fiona Ellingham, Fiona Iddon, Fiona Scott, G T Steel, the Gookey family, Graham Pentelow, Grumpy Givers, Helen Jones, Henry Yorke, Hilary Taylor, Holy Trinity Hazlemere, Ian Pickering, Irene Bom, Jacky Wise, Janet Gaukroger, Jeff Ffoulkes, Jennifer Boes, Jenny Webb, Jeremy Sharratt, Joel Payne, John and Sue Hargreaves, John Tasker, Jonathan Clark, Justin Blackett, Karen Turner, Keith Pickering, Lee Reddyhoff, Lincoln Baptist Church Selwyn (New Zealand), Linda Donaldson, Louise Franklin, Luke Middleton, Lydia,

Lynne Johnson, Maggie Forknell, Margaret Clark, Margaret Clarkson, Mark & Claire Ralf, Matt and Eils Osgood, Michael B Henderson, New City Church Milton Keynes, Nick Goldsworthy, Patricia Kibbler, Philip Nichols, Rev David Fleming, Richard and Diana Hutchins, Roger and Fiona Peach, Ryan Cartwright, Sally Baily, Sally Thornton, Sheena Williams, Stephen Sloss, St Michael's Chester Square, St Paul's Tervuren (Belgium), Stopsley Baptist Church, and Ulrike Hunt.

Thank you!

PART 1

CHAPTER 1

HOW WOULD JESUS LEAD WORSHIP?

We have worshipped to the beat of hand-drums in a Peruvian jungle, and with massed choirs in Canterbury Cathedral. We have sung alongside homeless, drug-addicted women in Luton, and suited millionaire business leaders in Cambridge. We have joined with Lutheran liturgy in Sweden, and Pentecostal praise in London. We have met God with toddlers in our local park, and with pensioners in our local parish church. What unites these experiences, these diverse groups? Not style. No single approach to music, or prayer, or service structure can bring harmony to these unlikely family members. What unites them is Jesus.

> Now in Christ Jesus you who once were far away
> have been brought near by the blood of Christ. For he
> himself is our peace, who has made the two groups
> one and has destroyed the barrier, the dividing wall of
> hostility. *(Ephesians 2:13-14)*

In an increasingly polarised world where people try to put up walls, troll their enemies and hide under their headphones, we desperately need some unity. And we won't find that unity by pushing a particular brand of worship style, or a one-size-fits all resource. Only Jesus can bring us together. Through Jesus, previously divided people 'come to the Father through the same Holy Spirit because of what Christ has done for us' (Ephesians 2:18 NLT).

If we say 'Jesus is our worship leader', what springs to your mind? Do you imagine Jesus with an acoustic guitar and a microphone, leading a band in his latest song? Or perhaps you picture him conducting a choir, or playing an organ, or guiding a congregation through a church service?

We like the question 'How would Jesus lead worship?' because it immediately reveals assumptions about what people think 'worship' is. Worship has become, for many people, the thing they do in church, or narrowed down further, to the thing they do as they sing certain songs. People talk about 'worship leaders', 'worship times' and 'worship spaces'.

Since we were teenagers we have been involved leading worship with songs. We've been employed by churches and trained teams across the UK to develop their music. We love to sing to God! But when we look to Jesus for his guidance in singing, we uncover just one Bible verse: 'When they had sung a hymn, they went out to the Mount of Olives' (Matthew 26:30).[1] This doesn't really feel like much to build a worship ministry on...

---

1   There is actually a bit more to the idea of Jesus singing than that. See the end of Chapter 2, and Michael O'Connor, 'The Singing of Jesus' in Begbie, Guthrie

I'LL BRING YOU MORE THAN A SONG

What if worship is *more than singing*? What if the whole, grand story of the Bible is concerned with a God who created people to worship him? The Bible uses a whole range of words which we translate or understand as 'worship' and most of them are not referring narrowly to music or singing.[2] We want to suggest that the following three terms might begin to sum up God's heart for worship. His desire is that all of humanity would:

> *Draw Near* - engage with God in close, reverent relationship;
> *Obey* - honour God by living his way; and
> *Glorify* - proclaim God's ways to the world.

We know that, sadly, the perfect relationship of worship which God intended in creation was broken.[3] Adam and Eve and the people of Israel failed to *Obey* God, their actions did not *Glorify* him and this resulted in not being able to *Draw Near*. And yet this gracious God made ways for his people to keep coming to him through the tabernacle, the priests and the sacrificial system.

Then, at the climax of his story, God stepped into our shoes. Jesus showed us what a life of worship *really* looked like. He lived the perfect life of *Drawing Near* to his Father,

---

(eds), *Resonant Witness* (Eerdmans, 2011) and Reggie Kidd, *With One Voice: Discovering Christ's Song in Our Worship* (Baker Books, 2005).

2   For a survey of biblical words for worship see David Peterson, *Engaging with God* (Apollos, 1992) pages 55–74.

3   Genesis 3, Romans 1:21.

Obeying God's will and bringing him *Glory* by the Holy Spirit. He fulfilled and exceeded the Old Testament system by becoming our eternal high priest and our once-for-all sacrifice. And through his life, death and resurrection he has made a way for us to worship with his kind of intimacy, obedience and confidence.

COMING BACK TO THE HEART OF WORSHIP

From this perspective, Jesus is not just someone we sing about, but the very heart of our worship. He is the one who shows us what true worship looks like, and he is the one who makes our worship possible. His life and ministry becomes the template for every life and every worship ministry. Not because he tells us how to choose songs or play the piano, but because he shows us what it means to *Draw Near*, *Obey* and *Glorify* our heavenly Father, in the power of the Holy Spirit. And he doesn't just demonstrate this for us to try and copy. He takes us by the hand and *leads us* into worship.

Is this a new idea to you? Do you find it intriguing, exciting, or are you scratching your head wondering where in the Bible we've got this from? To tackle these questions we will spend Chapter 2 unpacking the concept of Jesus as our worship leader. We'll have a particular focus on the letter to the Hebrews, and we'll delve into some theological treasures. It is a meaty chapter, and some people might be tempted to skip ahead to the more practical stuff in Chapters 3-6. Many worship teams and leaders want get on with the worshipping, rather than stand around talking about it. But we'd encourage

Zoe

, to reflect deeper on who Jesus is and so

ormed more and more into the likeness of

gradually becoming brighter and more beautiful as God enters our lives and we become like him. *(2 Corinthians 3:18 MSG)*

DOES OUR MUSIC MINISTRY MATTER?

Another question you might be asking is: If Jesus is the true worship leader, what does that mean for us as musicians, singers, service leaders, people who prepare and lead church services? If Jesus has made the 'new and living way' for us to come to God, does it even make a difference how we choose songs, or arrange music, or craft prayers? Does the way we lead when we gather on a Sunday matter?

This book is here to tell you that *your worship ministry matters.* In our work with engageworship we have spent the past decade travelling across the country, training and resourcing local church music teams. In every place, we see groups of (mostly) volunteer musicians and creatives, investing their precious time into church services. We get inspired by the commitment, pastoral care and creative energy which is poured into gathered worship week after week, and we believe that what you do makes a difference in the lives of your congregation. Not only that - the truth is that *God* delights in every offering made for him, every effort in leadership, every unseen bit of planning and administration.[4] The way you serve

---

4   1 Corinthians 15:58.

God by offering your gifts and talents matters to him, and we believe that he longs to see your worship ministry flourish.

The best Bible story we can think of to illustrate this is the offering of the loaves and fish.[5] The small boy prepared his little lunch and then carried it around the Sea of Galilee and up a mountain, as he followed Jesus and listened to his teaching. The few loaves and fish might have been enough for the boy, but they were clearly never going to be enough for all those thousands of people! Yet the boy offered them to Jesus. Jesus took them, blessed them, broke them, and gave them.[6] In the hands of Jesus, that small offering became *enough*.

In the same way, we as worship leaders come each week with what is in our hands: our few songs, our musical arrangements. We come with our prayers, our ideas for creative elements and service structures. They are the best we have, they might even be good. But they are never going to be enough to help every person in our church connect with God - it's not humanly possible to provide something that suits every single age, personality type, spiritual maturity and ability. And more than that, how could our small gifts and efforts be worthy of our Holy God? There are times when, like the disciples faced with more than 5000 hungry people, what we have feels deeply inadequate to the task at hand.

---

5   John 6:1-14.

6   The words used in Luke 9:16 - 'took, gave thanks, broke, gave' - are the same words Luke uses to describe Jesus' actions at the Lord's Supper (Luke 22:19). Luke mysteriously connects this boy's offering with Jesus' own offering of himself. Henri Nouwen expands on these four words 'taken, blessed, broken, given' in his book *Life of the Beloved,* and we turned this idea into a communion service. http://engageworship.org/TBBGcommunion

And yet, Jesus receives what is in our hands. He takes our offering, blesses it, breaks it, and gives it. When we offer our worship ministry through Jesus it becomes *enough*. It becomes worthy. It becomes significant.

Asking 'How would Jesus lead worship?' doesn't diminish the importance of singing and services. It expands it. The knowledge that ultimately *Jesus* draws us near to the Father by the Spirit doesn't cancel out the gifts and skills you bring. It humbles, perfects and elevates them to be of eternal significance.

BEYOND STYLE

Another good reason to focus on Jesus is that it helps us put to one side (at least for one blissful moment) arguments about worship *style*. A lot of discussion around worship centres on stylistic questions: Should we use hymns or songs? Screens or books? Agreed liturgy or improvised prayers? In-ear monitors or floor wedges? These are not irrelevant questions, but they are also not at the heart of what worship is really about.

You might want to think about worship styles being like clothing styles. Fashion choices are made based on culture and background, and people will attempt to express their personality through what they wear. Clothing is not irrelevant - there are culturally appropriate things to wear in different situations (for example, avoid t-shirts and shorts at a traditional funeral). But ultimately we know it is superficial to judge a person on their outward appearance. In a similar way, assessing worship simply on the basis of its outward style risks missing a deeper significance.

If someone says 'I want to be more like Jesus', we would be quite surprised to see them start dressing in a one-piece linen garment and sandals. That is not what we mean by 'being more like Jesus'.

Similarly, 'worshipping more like Jesus' doesn't mean taking a course in everyday Aramaic and learning some ancient Near Eastern scales and harmonies. Constance Cherry points out that Jesus engaged in a range of gathered worship practices relevant to his context:

> He was a worshipper from birth who consistently, even daily, worshipped at the temple and the synagogue, kept the Sabbath, spent much time in prayer, participated in the regular worship rituals [...] celebrated the Jewish annual festivals of worship, pronounced blessings upon people, sang the liturgy, preached, and taught in the temple and synagogue.[7]

The distinctive ways Jesus worshipped are important for us to look at, but the real challenge is to delve beyond the practices to see the principles and attitudes underneath. Christ-like worship for us today means grasping the heart of how Jesus honoured the Father by the Spirit in his day, and then expressing that faithfully in your context.

---

7   Constance Cherry, *Worship Like Jesus: A Guide For Every Follower* (Abingdon Press, 2019) page 5.

Christ-like worship ought to be 'indigenous' or 'incarnated' - expressed in stylistic and cultural forms which make sense to our community and the people we are trying to reach. The exciting thing is that this can take almost limitless forms, and be expressed in myriad ways. It has been our experience as we have travelled to a wide variety of churches, that Christ-like worship might look 'traditional' or, equally, 'contemporary' (whatever either of those words mean in your context). It can be loud or quiet, formal or spontaneous, highly visual or word-based. Rather than criticising or complaining about people who worship differently to us, we ought to celebrate the rich diversity of worship expressions across the world, and continue to expand our own tradition as we encounter new approaches. As worship historian James White puts it:

> The God whom we worship, after all, seems to relish diversity. If no two leaves of grass are the same and certainly no two people are identical, then it does not seem strange that there is so much variety in cultures. [...] Each culture will have its own contribution to make to the totality of Christian worship.[8]

This book is not asking you to change your culture or style, but to assess what you do in the light of Jesus' attitudes and values.

---

8   James F White, *A Brief History of Christian Worship* (Abingdon Press 1993), page 180.

WHAT DID JESUS DO?

We started leading worship back in the 1990s, a time in the Christian subculture when everybody knew what 'WWJD' stood for. The colourful wristbands encouraged us to think 'What Would Jesus Do?' about each situation. It is a good question, reflecting the biblical challenge 'Whoever claims to live in him must live as Jesus did' (1 John 2:5-6). But later, during our time at theological college, one of our lecturers (the wonderful, late Lish Eves) would challenge some interpretations of this slogan. She would say: 'the trouble with What Would Jesus Do is first you need to know what Jesus did!'

Of course, she was right. It is easy to justify anything with the comment 'that is how Jesus would do it'. You can co-opt Jesus into any scheme using that approach. So when we began asking 'How would Jesus lead worship?', we realised we would need to delve deep into the life of Jesus with fresh eyes. We focused on the Gospel of Luke, studying and reflecting on the character and attitudes of Jesus we found there. We then organised our thinking around four key points (used as headings for Chapters 3-6) which we have found useful in helping us encapsulate our findings. We saw Jesus modelling for us a life and ministry of someone who is a:

- Humble Servant
- Leader with Authority
- Creative Communicator
- Reliant on the Spirit

In Part 2 we will be unpacking where we see these in Jesus' life, and how they speak to worship ministry today. Our goal is to be both Jesus-centred but also practical, finding applications for how these things work out in church life.

These are the points which struck us after prayerfully studying Luke through the lens of worship. We have found them helpful for our own ministry and as we've taught them to church teams. As you begin to look at the gospels with the question 'How would Jesus lead worship?' in mind, you will probably come up with some different thoughts and categories.[9] In fact, we very much hope you will. Our aim is to get you thinking, discussing, and applying what you discover to your own church.

HOLDING TENSIONS

Although we might try to avoid it, tension is actually a hugely important creative force. Tension in a movie is what keeps the plot moving along. Tensions created by suspensions and cadences are what give shape to music. Even tuning an instrument like a piano, guitar or drum kit is an exercise in tension - pulling one thing against another to create a resonant, pleasing noise.

Often, Christian thinking about God requires holding ideas in tension. For example, in Chapter 2 we talk about the incarnation. When the early Church needed to formulate biblical truth into doctrine to avoid misunderstanding and heresy, they had to hold together two apparently opposite

---

9   For example see Cherry, *Worship Like Jesus*.

truths - that the incarnate Jesus was (and is) both fully God and fully human. We also talk in Chapter 2 about the Trinity - that in the Bible we clearly see one God who is three persons. The creeds do not allow us to collapse those tensions and, the more we delve into them, the more we will find that they give us life.

Many of our problems to do with worship in the contemporary church come from the collapse of tensions that should be held and celebrated. For example, we choose either the 'transcendence' of God, focusing on his power and majesty, or we cosy up to the 'immanent', intimate God, majoring on his love and grace. Instead, these attributes are supposed to be pulling against one another all the time. We need to proclaim and experience our God who is holy and beyond us, and yet at the same time makes himself known and available through his Son and Spirit.

Turning very practically to the ways we plan worship, think about the tensions between reaching seekers with easy-access gospel presentations (spiritual milk) and taking believers deeper in teaching and worship (spiritual meat).[10] Or the choice between hymns, with their depth of lyrical content but often low cultural relevance, and the contemporary but sometimes thematically lightweight songs. Or the 'we' of corporate worship versus the 'I' of personal response; planning versus spontaneity; quiet reflection versus noisy celebration.[11]

---

10   Hebrews 5:13-14.

11   For more examples of holding tensions in gathered worship, see Bob Kauflin, *Worship Matters: Leading Others to Encounter the Greatness of God* (Crossway, 2008) pages 153-210.

In Jesus, we see someone who does not fall for the temptation to collapse tensions. For example, he knows that his kingdom is not *of* this world,[12] yet he makes a difference to people *in* the world.[13] He came to save the whole of humankind, yet has time to stop with one individual.[14] He is the Lord of Lords, yet he came to serve.[15] His yoke is easy and his burden is light, yet he takes up his cross and calls us to do the same.[16]

Looking at the life of Jesus as a guide and model for our worship has helped us to see that we can often make false choices, narrowing down our worship style or practice to please ourselves or our congregations, when in fact Jesus calls us to hold things in tension and celebrate the differences. The chapter headings in Part 2 of this book pull against each other in very important ways: we are to follow Jesus' example in being 'Humble Servants' of our congregations and our communities, and at the same time we are called to be 'Leaders with Authority'. This might sound impossible, but Jesus shows us how. We are to develop our 'Creative Communication'; planning and rehearsing music, arts and other worship experiences fit for a king, and yet at the same time remain 'Reliant on the Spirit', not our own gifts, being adaptable and ready to change our plans at his leading. Jesus

---

12   John 18:36.

13   Luke 7:22.

14   As seen when he is on the way to heal a child but stops to speak to the woman who touches the hem of his robe - Mark 5:24–34.

15   Matthew 20:28.

16   Matthew 11:30; 16:24.

takes what is humanly impossible and shows how, with God, all things are possible.[17]

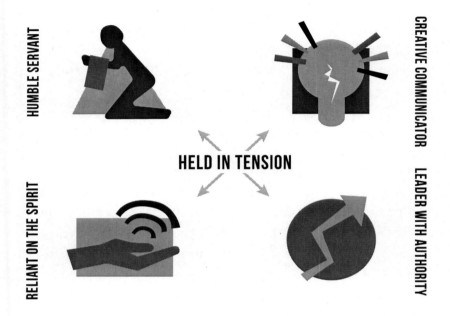

HUMBLE SERVANT

CREATIVE COMMUNICATOR

HELD IN TENSION

RELIANT ON THE SPIRIT

LEADER WITH AUTHORITY

USING THIS BOOK

We have created a video training course which can be used alongside this book. It is available entirely free online. We encourage you to take a look at the course and consider if you might run it with your team or some friends.[18]

If following the course, we suggest this reading plan:

---

17   Matthew 19:26.

18   https://engageworship.org/VideoCourse Here you will also find a free downloadable Leader's Guide with more information about how to run the sessions.

Session 1 - Read this chapter and Chapter 2 (Jesus our Worship Leader).

Session 2 - Read Chapter 3 (Humble Servant).

Session 3 - Read the first half of Chapter 4 (Leader with Authority) up to page 93.

Session 4 - Read the second half of Chapter 4, from pages 93 to 104.

Session 5 - Read Chapter 5 (Creative Communicator).

Session 6 - Read Chapter 6 (Reliant on the Spirit).

Alternatively, this book can be read without engaging with the videos. It is our aim that you grow both in understanding and practical experience as you read. Under the heading 'Ideas to Try' you will see, throughout the book, examples and suggestions for applying the teaching in corporate worship. The end of Chapter 2 presents a number of ideas as to how the theology can be applied in services. 'Leader with Authority' talks about how worship can be planned as a journey. 'Creative Communicator' is brimming with creative ideas for how to move worship beyond simply singing, and 'Humble Servant' looks at how we can fuse worship with social action. Finally, 'Reliant on the Spirit' gives practical tips for creating space to receive the Spirit and develop spontaneity.

We also want your experience of this book to be an act of worship in itself, so the heading 'Pause to Worship' is an invitation to put the book down and do some kind of activity to respond to God. It can be tempting to skip this kind of thing when you read a book, but give it a try and we pray that you will experience drawing closer to God. In fact, here is the first 'Pause to Worship' to finish this chapter.

● PAUSE TO WORSHIP

What is in your hands?

For Sam's birthday he received the gift of a hand-carved bread board, with a beautifully inscribed image in the top corner of five loaves and two fish. Rather than keep it in the kitchen, it sits on his desk. When he gets overwhelmed by life and worship ministry, he uses this board to help him come to God afresh.

Find a piece of paper and create your own simple drawing of five loaves and two fish. Reflect on the challenges in front of you when it comes to leading other people in worship. What is difficult? What feels impossible?

Then reflect on what God has put in your hands. What are your five loaves and two fish? What gifts, passions, opportunities or partnerships has God given to you? Write or draw them on your paper.

Think about how inadequate these gifts seem in the light of the needs you face. Choose to offer your gifts back to Jesus as the boy offered his loaves and fish. Allow Jesus to take, give thanks, break and give them.

Thank Jesus for receiving your gifts, for using them, for making them enough to lead his people in worship, in the power of the Holy Spirit.

CHAPTER 2

JESUS OUR WORSHIP LEADER

Do you ever worry that your worship isn't 'good' enough? That your songs, your singing or playing, or the way you lead the congregation is just not quite *enough* to bring people into the presence of God? Worship leader Bob Kauflin writes:

> I had a conversation once with a well-known worship leader who confessed that every time he leads worship, he experiences a great deal of anxiety. Will people 'get it'? Will they experience real worship?[19]

Do you ever feel like that? We know that *we* do. Or perhaps it goes deeper: your music and leading might be okay, but you fear that your life, your heart, your giving, your service, your sincerity - something about you, just isn't *enough* to allow you to truly worship God, or to lead other people in his praise. Again, you're not alone, we all feel like this at times. But this realisation is actually a good thing if it causes us to join with the Apostle Paul in saying:

I've tried everything and nothing helps. I'm at the
end of my rope. Is there no one who can do anything
for me? Isn't that the real question? The answer,
thank God, is that Jesus Christ can and does.
(Romans 7:24-25, MSG)

Our own efforts to reach God in worship will never be enough.
We can't, in our own strength, play, pray, sing or give our way
to God. Realising this is the first step towards the freedom and
transformation that comes from the greatest truth:

Jesus is enough.

IT'S ALL ABOUT JESUS

Often when people say something like 'Jesus is the heart of our
worship', they mean that we offer worship *to* Jesus and that we
focus on him during our times of singing. This is, of course,
entirely right and biblical. In the New Testament we see the
infant Jesus being worshipped by the Magi[20] and later by the
disciples.[21] Paul says that 'at the name of Jesus every knee
should bow'[22] and proclaims that Christ is God and for ever
praised.[23] In Revelation 5:12–13 we find a glorious picture of
Jesus, the Lamb of God, worshipped for eternity along with
God the Father.

At the same time, we need to hold this in tension with
another important New Testament emphasis: prayer and

---

20   Matthew 2:11.
21   Matthew 28:17; Luke 5:8; John 20:28.
22   Philippians 2:10.
23   Romans 9:5.

worship addressed *to* the Father *through* the Son.[24] The New Testament speaks of us worshipping *in the name of* Jesus,[25] and even worshipping *with* Jesus.[26] This leads theologian James Torrance to write:

> Jesus Christ is the leader of our worship, and leads us into the holy presence of the Father [...] He is the one true Priest, the one true worshipper, the leader of our worship [...] through whom alone we can draw near to God.[27]

For us, the idea that Jesus is the true worship leader has revolutionised the way we approach worship music and church services. It tells us that not only were we *saved* by grace through the work of Christ, but that we continue to offer prayers, songs and other acts of worship *only* by the grace of God, through the work of Christ. It is not about us - it is all about Jesus. It is not about what we can *do* in worship - but what Jesus had already *done*. Can you see how freeing this could be? How grace-drenched? How encouraging?

---

24   See for example Romans 1:8; Hebrews 13:15 and 1 Peter 1:3. This was highlighted by Josef A. Jungmann in his 1925 work, *The Place of Christ in Liturgical Prayer*. See also Bryan D. Spinks (ed.) *The Place of Christ in Liturgical Prayer: Trinity, Christology and Liturgical Theology* (Pueblo, 2008).

25   Ephesians 5:20; Colossians 3:17.

26   Ephesians 2:5-6; Colossians 3:1; Hebrews 2:12.

27   James B Torrance, *Worship, Community and the Triune God of Grace* (IVP Academic, 1996), pages 47, 53–54.

THE CONSUMING FIRE OF GOD'S LIGHT

One of our key terms for worship in Chapter 1 was *Drawing Near*. Leaders of contemporary worship will often talk of coming into God's presence. But thinking that *we* can achieve this in our own strength goes entirely against the picture the Bible paints for worship:

> Biblically speaking, no worship leader, pastor, band, or song will ever bring us close to God. We can't shout, dance, or prophesy our way into God's presence. Worship itself cannot lead us into God's presence.[28]

We learn from Genesis 3 and know from our own experience that human selfishness causes a breakdown in the relationship between God and humans. This makes us sinful, 'unholy'. And one of the central problems of Old Testament worship is this: if an unholy people come into contact with the holy God, the result can only be certain death.[29] Unholy and holy cannot co-exist, much like darkness and light. Imagine a completely dark, windowless room. As soon as you open the door even the tiniest crack, the darkness is no more. It has been annihilated. It's instantaneous.

We are all 'infected' by the disease of sin, which leads to death.[30] God's holiness is a 'consuming fire',[31] obliterating any unholiness it encounters. This makes it impossible for us to

---

28   Kauflin, *Worship Matters*, pages 73–74.
29   Exodus 33:20; Leviticus 10:1–3; 1 Chronicles 13:9–10.
30   Romans 5:12.
31   Hebrews 12:29.

come to God in our own strength, and poses a big problem for worship: Would many people be attracted to our churches if certain death was on the order of service, just after the notices?

GOD BEHIND THE CURTAIN

Hebrews 9:1-5 tells how God made gracious provision for the people of Israel to come and worship him. It describes the sacred space that God set aside - the Tabernacle (an early portable version of the Temple).

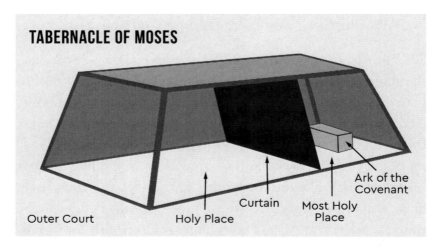

TABERNACLE OF MOSES

Ark of the Covenant

Curtain

Most Holy Place

Outer Court   Holy Place

There was an outer court, where the ordinary people could come. Then there was the Holy Place, where the priests could go to offer sacrifices. These priests were the closest thing the Old Testament had to 'worship leaders' - people who would bring the worship of the people to God. Finally, behind a thick curtain, was the Most Holy Place, or Holy of Holies, where

God's presence on earth rested above the Ark of the Covenant. The writer goes on to say:

> Only the high priest entered the inner room, and that only once a year, and never without blood, which he offered for himself and for the sins the people had committed in ignorance. *(Hebrews 9:7)*

Coming into God's presence was serious business. The first high priest received a severe warning from God:

> 'Tell your brother Aaron not to come whenever he chooses into the Most Holy Place behind the curtain in front of the atonement cover on the ark, or else he will die, because I appear in the cloud over the atonement cover.' *(Leviticus 16:2)*

Leviticus 16 goes on to explain how the high priest is to enter the Most Holy Place once a year, the high point of Israel's worship called the Day of Atonement. There he would offer two goats for the sins of the people, after first making many preparations and burning incense to protect him from God's presence.[32] Note the seriousness of sin here, and the lengths God will go to to enable his people to draw near.

A NEW AND LIVING WAY

Knowing this, it should shock us, as it must have profoundly shocked the first readers, to see the writer to the Hebrews say:

---

32   For more on the Day of Atonement and Jesus' fulfilment of it see Torrance, *Worship, Community and the Triune God of Grace*, pages 47-50.

> Therefore, brothers and sisters, since we have
> *confidence to enter the Most Holy Place* by the blood
> of Jesus, by a *new and living way* opened for us
> through the curtain, that is, his body, and since we
> have a great priest over the house of God, let us *draw*
> *near to God* with a sincere heart in full assurance of
> faith, having our hearts sprinkled to cleanse us from a
> guilty conscience and having our bodies washed with
> pure water. *(Hebrews 10:19–22, emphasis added)*

Can you imagine the reaction to this? 'We know that entering the Most Holy Place means death! How can we have confidence to draw near to God: we are unholy, he is holy?' The writer to the Hebrews is happy to respond with two world-changing reasons.

Firstly, Jesus' blood, shed for us on the cross, opens up a 'new and living way' into God's presence, far superior to the blood of the goat on the Day of Atonement. In Luke 23:44–46 we read that, at the moment Jesus died, the curtain separating the people - us - from the Holy of Holies and the presence of God, was torn in two from top to bottom. The way was made open for each one of us, however unworthy, to enter, not a room in a tent or a temple, but the heavenly reality of which the Old Testament system was only a picture - the presence of our loving Father.

Secondly, we have a new high priest, one who is far superior to the Old Testament priests, who offered the sacrifice of his own blood for us. Jesus takes the role of both sacrifice *and* high priest, uniquely offering himself as the once-for-all solution to the problem of sin. Jesus is our eternal high priest, our ultimate worship leader, who has opened up the way for us to draw near to God.

TWO SIDES OF JESUS: 1. HIS HUMANITY

It may be that your mind is already blown by this idea, in which case feel free to pause and praise God for what he has done for us in Jesus! But it might be that this teaching is just opening up *more* questions for you. Like - how come only Jesus can do this for us? What makes him uniquely qualified to lead us into the presence of God? To tackle these questions we come into contact with two huge and exciting concepts: Jesus' humanity (or the 'doctrine of the Incarnation'), and Jesus' God-ness (or the 'doctrine of the Trinity').

Jesus' coming to earth as a human is explained in Hebrews using the image of an Old Testament high priest. It explains that:

> Every high priest is selected from among the people
> and is appointed to represent them in matters related
> to God, to offer gifts and sacrifices for sins. He is able
> to deal gently with those who are ignorant and are
> going astray, since he himself is subject to weakness.
> *(Hebrews 5:1–2)*

Remember, the high priest was the closest figure in the Old Testament to a worship leader, fully aware of his own humanity and weakness as he presented the people's worship to God. Jesus, to become our Great High Priest and save us through his sacrifice, had to become fully human:

> Since the children have flesh and blood, he too shared
> in their humanity so that by his death he might break
> the power of him who holds the power of death [...] For
> this reason he had to be made like them, fully human
> in every way, in order that he might become a merciful
> and faithful high priest in service to God, and that
> he might make atonement for the sins of the people.
> *(2:14, 17)*

It is an ancient yet enduring heresy that Jesus was just *pretending* to be human. It is as if we imagine he's like Clark Kent, wearing human clothes and bumbling around pretending to be normal, yet under it all he was really a kind of Superman. The writer to the Hebrews is deeply concerned that we should not make this mistake. The Christian faith has always affirmed that the incarnate Jesus was fully God and yet also fully human - one of those creative tensions that we described in Chapter 1. We need to hold tight to both Jesus' humanity and his God-ness, not choosing one over the other but allowing them to pull against each other and shape our understanding of him.

Born a human being just like us, Jesus faced the same struggles that we do, but remained faithful to God. He was 'tempted in every way, just as we are - yet was without sin' (4:15). Part of our definition of worship is to '*Obey* - honour God by living his way'. Jesus is the perfect example of somebody entirely devoted to living out the Father's will.[33] He shows us what it means to be fully human, fully alive, fully glorifying God.

The writer to the Hebrews explains that the blood of bulls and goats could not save people fully. It could not provide lasting purification of body and soul.[34] In the end, humanity had to die for its own sin. The problem is, as sinful beings, we could not be the spotless sacrifice that was required. Only Jesus, by living according to the Father's will as a perfect human being, could take our place. On the cross, his sacrifice dealt with death for ever and made us holy. His life of perfect worship makes our worship possible.[35]

💡 IDEAS TO TRY

Jesus' humanity

In recognising the significance of Jesus' humanity, we should take a fresh look at our church services. We may tend to sing only about the risen, exalted Jesus, while neglecting to celebrate his earthly life. If Jesus' humanity was real, genuine flesh and blood, then he was born with the same weakness and need for teaching and development that are common to us all.[36] His hunger and thirst would have been genuine.[37] He would

---

33   John 5:36.
34   Hebrews 9:9, 13; 10:3–4.
35   Hebrews 5:7–10; 10:8–10.
36   Luke 2:41–52.
37   Matthew 21:18; John 19:28.

have got properly tired.[38] Jesus affirms the essential goodness of our humanity; redeemed and made perfect in him. Gathered worship in this context should be not only focused on the heavenlies but also rooted in our everyday lives.

Have you been involved in worship that celebrates our human experiences in the light of Jesus? Do we offer people the comfort that Jesus knows what it is like to be human, to struggle, to be tempted? You could look at songs such as Sam's all-age 'Jesus You Know What it's Like',[39] Audrey Assad's 'Humble',[40] or the Porter's Gate's 'Wood and Nails'.[41] Engaging with Jesus' humanity is a largely untapped theme for congregations, and an area where we fail to give Jesus full credit and glory.

☀ IDEAS TO TRY

Jesus and emotions

Jesus' humanity can also be an encouragement to engage with a wider range of human emotions. Jeremy Begbie writes that in response to the worship leadership of the incarnate Jesus:

> Christ assumed the whole of our humanness in order to redeem us. Included in this are our *emotions*, likewise our renewal in his image. Emotions are [...]

---

38   John 4:6.
39   https://engageworship.org/ideas/jesus-you-know
40   https://engageworship.org/HWJlinks
41   https://engageworship.org/HWJlinks

part of what God desires to transform, not least in worship. At its best, then, worship is a school of the emotions.[42]

Consider how you can include a wider range of emotions in your gathered worship. How could you help a congregation express pure joy,[43] or righteous anger,[44] or anguished sorrow?[45] Find songs that express a range of emotions and experiences, such as 'Christ be in My Waking',[46] 'Weep With Me'[47] or 'Blessed Be Your Name'.[48] Use the actual names of emotions as you lead prayer, for example, 'We feel angry when we see this injustice' or 'We feel sad when we read this news.'

● PAUSE TO WORSHIP

Jesus' hands, your hands

Look at your hands. Examine your fingers, the creases, the nails, the dirt. Think about the fact that Jesus had flesh and blood, male hands - not the marble or plaster of a statue. They were probably a bit more worn than yours, perhaps dirtier, but they had skin, bones, nails. Imagine what Jesus' hands might have looked like when

42   Jeremy S Begbie 'Faithful Feelings', in Begbie, Guthrie (eds) *Resonant Witness* page 337.
43   Luke 10:21.
44   Luke 19:45-46.
45   Luke 22:44.
46   By Stuart Townend and Simon Brading. https://engageworship.org/HWJlinks
47   By Rend Collective. https://engageworship.org/HWJlinks
48   By Beth and Matt Redman. https://engageworship.org/HWJlinks

he reached out to touch someone, to heal a leper, when he broke bread at the last supper, when he washed the disciples' feet. He had flesh-and-blood hands.

Reflect on this passage:

> In bringing many sons and daughters to glory, it was fitting that God, for whom and through whom everything exists, should make the pioneer of their salvation perfect through what he suffered. Both the one who makes people holy and those who are made holy are of the same family. So Jesus is not ashamed to call them brothers and sisters. He says,

> 'I will declare your name to my brothers and sisters; in the assembly I will sing your praises.' [...]

> Since the children have flesh and blood, he too shared in their humanity so that by his death he might break the power of him who holds the power of death - that is, the devil - and free those who all their lives were held in slavery by their fear of death. [...] For this reason he had to be made like them, fully human in every way, in order that he might become a merciful and faithful high priest in service to God, and that he might make atonement for the sins of the people. Because he himself suffered when he was tempted, he is able to help those who are being tempted. (Hebrews 2:10-12, 14-15, 17-18)

How are you feeling right now? Spend a moment thinking about it. Are you thirsty, happy, tired, exhausted, aching, sleepy? Remember, Jesus has experienced all those feelings, and bigger emotions too - love, loneliness, joy, despair, even guilt and shame on the cross. He calls you his sister or brother; he knows how you feel. Why not spend a moment now, talking to him about it?

TWO SIDES OF JESUS: 2. HIS GOD-NESS

So far, we have looked at how Jesus solved the problem of unholy people coming into the presence of God, by offering himself, as both sacrifice and high priest, on the cross. Part of the reason why Jesus was uniquely qualified to do this was that he lived a fully human life of obedient worship. But what about the fact that he was fully God? What impact does that have on our worship? The writer to the Hebrews addresses this at the very beginning of the letter.

> ... in these last days he has spoken to us by his Son, whom he appointed heir of all things, and through whom he made the universe. The Son is the radiance of God's glory and the exact representation of God's being, sustaining all things by his powerful word. *(Hebrews 1:2–3a)*

As we can see here, the writer is very concerned to show that Jesus is far more than a prophet or an angel. If you need any more convincing, look at verse 6: 'And again, when God brings his firstborn into the world, he says, "Let all God's angels worship him."'

It may seem quite normal for us to think of Jesus as deserving worship, but it would have been scandalous to the original hearers. Central to Israel's faith was the conviction that God was *one*[49] and that no one else could share his worship. As good Jews, Jesus' first followers believed passionately that there was one God. They knew that Jesus was not himself the Father. Yet we've also seen that they knew and worshipped Jesus as God. Although they may not have argued over the finer points or written them up as a detailed creed, the New Testament Christians bore witness to Jesus as God, and to the Father as God.

They also began to see the intimate connection between the Father, the Son and a third person, the Holy Spirit. They grasped that the incarnate Jesus was, unlike us, perfectly filled with the Holy Spirit from birth to do the will of the Father. John the Baptist says of him that he has been given 'the Spirit without limit' (John 3:34), and Jesus himself explains that he 'can do nothing by himself; he can do only what he sees his Father doing' (5:19). In his conception, baptism, preaching, miracles, worship and in other points of his earthly life, Jesus was empowered by the Holy Spirit to do the will of the Father.[50] His life and worship are our clearest example of what became known as the doctrine of the Trinity.[51]

---

49   Deuteronomy 6:4.

50   We will delve further into examples of this in Chapter 6, and its implications for how we lead worship.

51   We obviously don't have room here to explore this subject as much as we would like. A very readable introduction to the Trinity in reference to worship is Robin Parry, *Worshipping Trinity* (Paternoster Press, 2005). For something a bit more weighty, try Christopher Cocksworth, *Holy, Holy, Holy* (Apollos 1992).

The first Christians began to grasp the concept of one God and three persons because they experienced it in their worship. They drew near to God the Father through the life, death and resurrection of the Son, in the power of the Holy Spirit. And they did this because they had first seen it modelled in the life of Jesus, as he lived in intimate relationship with his Father, by the Holy Spirit.

ABBA - KNOWING ME, KNOWING YOU (A-HA)

One example of this intimacy can be seen in Jesus' use of the word *Abba*,[52] a word that, according to some scholars, had never been used before by Israelites to refer to God, as it was far too intimate and familiar. Jesus, in using it freely, was demonstrating a 'relationship with God of unique intimacy and intensity'.[53]

The truly amazing fact is that we, too, can be filled and empowered by the same Holy Spirit, to worship the Father along with Jesus:

> Because you are his children, God sent the Spirit of his Son into our hearts, the Spirit who calls out, '*Abba*, Father'. *(Galatians 4:6, see also Romans 8:14-17)*

Because of what Jesus has done on the cross, we are adopted by God as daughters and sons.[54] God puts his Spirit in our hearts so that, just as Jesus did, we can enter into that intimate

---

52   Mark 14:36.

53   Cocksworth, *Holy, Holy, Holy*, page 33.

54   Ephesians 1:5.

relationship, calling God *Abba*, drawing close to our loving heavenly Father.

As James Torrance puts it, worship is not 'what we, religious people, do to try to please God' but instead, 'worship is the gift of grace to participate through the Spirit in the incarnate Son's communion with the Father - the way of joy and peace and confidence.'[55] Our worship becomes far more than singing some songs or saying some words to a distant God who we hope might hear us, if we do it well enough. It becomes the free gift of sharing in Jesus' worship and relationship with the Father, by the Spirit.

THE JESUS FILTER

The implications for our worship today are profound. Not only has Jesus shown us how to live a life of perfect worship, not only has he made the 'new and living way' for us to worship by his sacrifice, and not only has he invited us to share in his relationship with the Father, but he also continues to offer our praise to God right now. To say 'Jesus is our worship leader' means not only that he has opened the way to the Father in the past, but that right now he 'lives to intercede' for us as we worship the Father through Christ, by the Spirit.[56]

We, the people who call ourselves worship leaders, are not the mediators between the people and God. That role belongs to Jesus.[57] It is not up to us to 'make something happen', to create an atmosphere or attempt to generate a response.

---

55   Torrance, *Worship*, page 59.

56   Hebrews 7:25.

57   1 Timothy 2:5; Hebrews 8:6.

Humans will always try to reach God with their own efforts, or via another mediator. It is easy to criticise those who try to reach God through religious ritual, statues of idols, superstitions or other such things. But we can lose sight of the fact that the modern music and 'worship leader' model so popular in the contemporary church can become just as much an idol, a false-mediator, a replacement for Jesus. Harold Best writes:

> There is only one way to God, through Jesus Christ. This means that God sees and hears all of our offerings perfected. God sees and hears as no human being can, all because our offerings have been perfected by the giver. The out-of-tune singing of an ordinary believer [...] the nearly transcendent 'Kyrie' of Bach's B Minor Mass, the praise choruses of the charismatic, the drum praise of the Cameroonian - everything from the widow's mite to the poured-out ointment of artistic action - are at once humbled and exalted by the strong saving work of Christ.[58]

Have you ever thought about that? That each act of worship you bring is simultaneously *humbled* and *exalted* in Christ? Every song, prayer and act of service passes through a kind of 'Jesus filter', and is both shown as terminally inadequate while at the same time made beautifully complete in him.

---

58   Harold Best, *Music Through the Eyes of Faith* (HarperCollins, 1993) pages 155-56.

This is the 'wonderful exchange'... by which Christ
takes what is ours (our broken lives and unworthy
prayers), sanctifies them, offers them without spot or
wrinkle to the Father.[59]

This should bring us freedom and encouragement as we
partner with Christ, by the Spirit, to lead our congregations
in worship. We will never get ourselves 'right' enough to offer
sufficient worship to God. No amount of practice, creativity,
effort or planning can force a way into the presence of the
Father. Yet in his mercy he has made a way: in Christ we can
offer acceptable worship by the Spirit.

⚡ IDEAS TO TRY

Worship through Jesus

There are ways of letting these Trinitarian perspectives
on worship permeate your times of corporate praise.
Introducing them in gathered services will help you
move beyond an intellectual understanding into a lived
experience of worshipping the Father, through the Son,
in the Holy Spirit.

One simple way of doing this is by drawing people's
attention (perhaps at the start of a time of singing) to
the fact that we worship through Christ, perhaps by
reading the following scripture or having everyone read
it together:

---

59 Torrance, *Worship, Community and the Triune God of Grace*, page 15.

'Through Jesus, therefore, let us continually offer to God a sacrifice of praise - the fruit of lips that confess his name' *(Hebrews 13:15).*

Similarly, you can remind people of the image of the curtain in the temple, and how Jesus' death has torn this curtain in two, allowing us to enter into the presence of God. To help them picture it, you can read Hebrews 10:19–22 and perhaps even set up a visual aid of a curtain, which can be torn down or flung back.

Most of us will be familiar with singing about Jesus as the sacrificial lamb killed in our place. How often, though, do we sing about or identify Jesus in our worship as our high priest, our mediator, our one and only way to God the Father? One notable example of a song based on this theme is 'Before the Throne of God Above'.[60] You could use this hymn and encourage people to reflect on Jesus as the one who intercedes for us in heaven. Alternatively, Sam's round 'Jesus Lead us to the Father'[61] and Andy Irons' 'Father God We Come'[62] both have texts that engage us with the Trinitarian dynamic of worship.

---

60   https://engageworship.org/HWJlinks
61   https://engageworship.org/HWJlinks
62   https://engageworship.org/HWJlinks

🕐 PAUSE TO WORSHIP

Singing with Jesus

Can you imagine Jesus singing? Can you imagine him leading you in song? It is true that the forms of music he would have used in his earthly life would sound very alien to us, but it remains the case that Jesus sang when he was with his disciples.[63] He grew up with the psalms and the singing of synagogue worship.[64] The words of psalms were on his lips when he died on the cross, and some have suggested it might have been more natural for Jesus to express this in a form of singing:

> At the darkest moment of the cross, Jesus was not reduced to silence, but the musical moan of Psalm 22, 'My God, my God, why have you forsaken me?'[65]

Jesus turns to Psalm 22 in his death, but the New Testament also applies it to his resurrection. The writer to the Hebrews puts Psalm 22:22 on the lips of the risen Jesus:

> So Jesus is not ashamed to call them brothers and sisters. He says, 'I will declare your name to my brothers and sisters; in the assembly I will sing your praises.' (Hebrews 2:11-12)

---

63   Matthew 26:30.

64   Michael O'Connor, 'The Singing of Jesus' in Begbie, Guthrie (eds), *Resonant Witness*, pages 435-436.

65   Paul Westermeyer, *Te Deum: The Church and Music*, (Fortress, 1998), pages 39-40. See also Kidd, *With One Voice*, chapters 4-6.

There is a rich history of interpreting this passage to say that Jesus leads us in singing.[66] John Calvin wrote:

> And it is a truth, which may serve as a most powerful stimulant, and may lead us most fervently to praise God, when we hear that Christ leads our songs, and is the chief composer of our hymns.[67]

Take a moment to meditate on what it would mean to join with Jesus in singing. Do you go along with Calvin in being excited by the idea that Jesus 'leads our songs and is the chief composer of our hymns'? Does it change the way you think of approaching gathered worship, to know that Jesus is the senior worship leader, the true lead singer, who invites you to partner with him in leading the congregation? Can you imagine in your mind's eye what that would look like, as you joined with Jesus in singing praise to the Father, by the Spirit?

66 For a thorough look at Jesus as worship leader in Hebrews 2:12, see Ron Man, *Proclamation and Praise* (Wipf and Stock, 2007).

67 *Commentaries on the Epistle to the Hebrews by John Calvin*, pages 66-67, quoted in O'Connor, 'Singing', pages 441-442.

PART 2

CHAPTER 3

HUMBLE SERVANT

The child grew and became strong; he was filled with wisdom, and the grace of God was on him. *(Luke 2:40)*

The opening chapters of Luke's gospel trace Jesus' steady development from his humble birth. Luke says that Jesus grew in wisdom, in favour with God and the people,[68] and this culminates in the high point of his baptism at around 30 years of age.[69] The baptism is a proper 'mountaintop' moment, as heaven opens, the Holy Spirit descends and the Father speaks words of love and affirmation. What a beginning to a life of ministry!

When a monarch is crowned, a sports personality signs to a new team, or a business leader is made CEO, we expect this kind of ceremony to launch them into a successful and dynamic career. We might assume that Jesus will step out of the river and immediately begin to preach and heal, to capitalise

---

68   Luke 2:52.
69   Luke 3:21-23.

on this moment by growing his fan-base and fulfilling his mission. And yet, what is the very next thing that happens?

> Jesus, full of the Holy Spirit, left the Jordan and was led by the Spirit into the wilderness, where for forty days he was tempted by the devil. *(Luke 4:1-2)*

He appears to go from hero to zero. Man-of-the-moment to loner in the desert. Mountaintop joy to valley-of-the-shadow struggle. If the story so far has been a steady rise in prominence, success and affirmation, suddenly the graph seems to take a nose dive. And yet, notice that this was not a mistake or a punishment - Jesus is led *by the Holy Spirit* into this time of testing, trial and trouble. For him, success was not about crowds or results. It was about obedience and humility.

How do you rate a successful worship ministry? Does the unspoken worship leaders' pecking order go something like this:

1. International touring worship megastar
2. Most views on YouTube, or streams on Spotify
3. Leads worship at national conferences
4. Employed by a church to lead worship
5. Has some songs published
6. Leads worship regularly with a great band
7. Leads in a small church with a struggling music group
8. Occasionally plays in the band
9. On the sound desk rota
10. Leads the music when everybody else is on holiday...

Be honest, have you ever slotted yourself into an order like this? It is our fallen human nature that considers success to mean fame, power and recognition - precisely the opposite of the humility Jesus demonstrates.

How we define 'success' as a worship leader is an essential issue for us, and we should take heart from the knowledge that, throughout his ministry, Jesus had to wrestle with similar matters. 'What does it mean to be the Son of God?' and 'What kind of Messiah am I?' were vital questions for Jesus to resolve, and the first was never posed more clearly than in his battle with the devil in the wilderness.

TITLES AND TEMPTATIONS

Jesus' 40 days are intended to remind us of Israel's 40 years in the wilderness, and his tests and temptations are likened to those of Israel in the desert.[70] This is highlighted by the fact that, in answering all three temptations, Jesus quotes from Deuteronomy,[71] passages that relate to Israel's wilderness testing.

So in one sense, Jesus was being tempted as a representative of Israel, and of fallen humankind. His temptations reflect the kind of testing we all go through. He succeeds where we fail. This means we can relate to these temptations, and learn from Jesus' example in our worship ministry.

Take the first one:

---

70   I. Howard Marshall, *New International Greek Testament Commentary, Luke* (Paternoster Press, 1978), page 166.
71   Deuteronomy 8:3; 6:13 and 6:16.

> The devil said to him, 'If you are the Son of God, tell
> this stone to become bread.' *(Luke 4:3)*

Now, there is nothing inherently wrong in making or eating
bread. So what is the potential sin here? Look how the devil
sets it up: *'If* you are the Son of God'. This is a temptation
for Jesus to justify himself - his identity, his role. The devil is
saying, 'Prove it!' Have you ever heard that voice in your head?

'*If* you are the worship leader, make your church
worship!'

'*If* you are a songwriter, write some worship hits!'

'*If* you are a success at what you do, demand more pay,
power and recognition!'

Sometimes, we can do something that is neutral or good
(like making bread, or leading worship in a certain way), but
with the wrong motivations. We do it to prove ourselves. We
can be tempted to justify our position by using God-given gifts
for selfish reasons. Joel Green says of this passage:

> [The devil] starts by urging Jesus to use his power in
> his own way to serve his own ends; he thus reinterprets
> 'Son of God' to mean the opposite of faithful
> obedience.[72]

Did you see that - the devil *reinterprets* 'Son of God'; he
defines it in a way contrary to God's will and purpose. How
often do we allow ourselves to reinterpret 'worship leader' as
something that is the opposite of 'faithful obedience'?

72   Joel Green, *New International Commentary on the New Testament: Luke*
(Eerdmans, 1997), page 192.

A whole industry has grown up around worship music and worship leaders over the last few decades. It has taken its cue from the celebrity culture and music industry around us, and redefined what it means to be a worship leader. What perhaps starts as a well-intentioned desire to share some good songs, snowballs into tracking YouTube views, hiring stylists and being sucked into a PR machine. Only a few people will reach the heights of this industry, but the same attitudes can trickle down as far as average Sunday morning worship times. We find it important to regularly check our attitudes and actions, to see if 'worship leader' has become for us something other than a humble servant of God and the congregation.

WHAT PATH TO 'SUCCESS'?

The second temptation has an even greater connection with our approach to worship:

> The devil led him up to a high place and showed him in an instant all the kingdoms of the world. And he said to him, 'I will give you all their authority and splendour; it has been given to me, and I can give it to anyone I want to. If you worship me, it will all be yours.' Jesus answered, 'It is written: "Worship the Lord your God and serve him only."' *(Luke 4:5-8)*

Jesus would have been aware of prophecies which told of the Messiah being sovereign over all the nations.[73] He was destined

---

73   See Psalm 2:8, Luke 1:33.

by God to be 'successful'. So why should he not just go for that success straight away?

Jesus knew that the path to the fulfilment of his calling was not the easy route but the hard way. He was not going to take the nations by force, by superior firepower. He was called to walk the path of humility, of service, of self-sacrifice. His road led not to a palace with a throne (or a stadium with a stage and a light show), but to a hill with a cross.

Jesus knew, too, that if he went along any other route, he would be taking the glory away from God. 'Worshipping the devil' is easier than we might think: you don't have to sacrifice virgins or play heavy metal records backwards. Any form of idolatry, putting anything - your instrument, your ministry, your creativity, human applause and recognition - before God is a way of worshipping the one who tempts you to do so. The Israelites in the wilderness were amazingly quick to forget God and worship idols[74] and often, so are we. Yet Jesus knew that there is only one who deserves our worship. He refused to achieve 'success' in his ministry by taking the easy road offered to him by the devil, because he knew this was a form of idolatry.

There have been times when we have found ourselves on a 'high place' - when services or events we have led worship at seem to have gone really well, or we have had some other human accolade. Those are the moments when the temptation to idolise 'success' becomes very real. There is also the risk that at those moments, when we're high on endorphins, we start

---

74   Exodus 32:1-6.

taking short-cuts to further exaltation, to get another hit of human affirmation. It's important - at all times, but especially in times of 'success' - to surround ourselves with friends that we can be accountable to. They help us to stay grounded and remind us that it is only God who deserves the glory.

TESTING, TESTING, 1,2,3

The third temptation places Jesus at the highest point of the temple - probably the royal colonnade, which overlooked a deep ravine.[75] The devil has been thwarted by scripture twice, so now he tries his own quotation:

> 'If you are the Son of God,' he said, 'throw yourself down from here. For it is written: "He will command his angels concerning you to guard you carefully; they will lift you up in their hands, so that you will not strike your foot against a stone."' *(Luke 4:9-11)*

This is interesting because, within the space of a few verses,[76] Jesus *is* saved by God from being thrown off a cliff. Of course, God can be trusted to fulfil his promises, but Jesus knew that he was not to test God or his own powers by doing something stupid with the underlying motive of drawing attention to himself. He replied simply, 'It says: "Do not put the Lord your God to the test"' (4:12).

Not many of us will be tempted to leap from the roof of St Paul's Cathedral, but we might do something not dissimilar

---

75   Marshall, *Luke*, page 172.
76   Luke 4:29-30.

in terms of leading worship. For example, do we ever loudly proclaim that we haven't bothered to plan anything for a worship time, trying to make ourselves look spiritual and 'testing' God by expecting him to lead us anyway? Have you ever taken a 'leap of faith' which was more about getting attention than following God's will? Or perhaps we expect healing or other miracles in church services, not out of compassion for the sick but because we hope they will bolster our own ego and ministry?

In each of these temptations, Jesus has a choice about the definition of his role as the Son of God. Does the title mean someone powerful, performing crowd-pleasing miracles and ruling over the world by force and might? Each time, Jesus chooses to say, 'No'. Instead, he chooses to define the Son of God as one who is obedient, humble and self-sacrificing.

As we define 'worship leader', which path will we choose?

WHO DO YOU SAY I AM?

> Once when Jesus was praying in private and his disciples were with him, he asked them, 'Who do the crowds say I am?' They replied, 'Some say John the Baptist; others say Elijah; and still others, that one of the prophets of long ago has come back to life.' 'But what about you?' he asked. 'Who do you say I am?' Peter answered, 'The Christ of God.' Jesus strictly warned them not to tell this to anyone. *(Luke 9:18–21)*

We read words such as 'Messiah' and 'Christ' today - the Hebrew and Greek terms for 'the anointed one' - and think of them in the light of Jesus. We associate them with the Son of God, with his divinity, with his dying on a cross. But for Jesus' contemporaries, their hope in a coming Messiah involved very different preconceptions. The place where they lived was occupied territory, and people were looking out for a political revolutionary, a military deliverer who could conquer the Romans by force.

This was in sharp contrast to Jesus' own definition of Messiah. Once his identity was out in the open, he was forced to redefine it radically for the disciples. If they were expecting a conquering hero-king, they were going to be disappointed. In a stunning piece of expectation management, Jesus turns their idea of Messiah on its head: 'The Son of Man must suffer many things and be rejected by the elders, chief priests and teachers of the law, and he must be killed and on the third day be raised to life' (9:22).

We can perhaps imagine the disciples' perplexed faces, the sick feeling in their stomachs, their incredulity at what Jesus is suggesting. A suffering Messiah? Rejected by the religious leaders? Killed and then resurrected? Surely Jesus was using metaphorical language again; he could not mean this literally!

FINDING THE REAL YOU

Immediately after redefining the concept of Messiah, Jesus goes on to recast what it looks like to be a *follower* of the Messiah. 'Whoever wants to be my disciple must deny themselves and take up their cross daily and follow me' (Luke 9:23). Jesus' first hearers knew what 'taking up your cross' meant. As Leon Morris explains,

> When a man from one of their villages took up a cross and went off with a little band of Roman soldiers, he was on a one-way journey. He would not be back. Taking up the cross meant the utmost in self denial.[77]

This is a challenge not just to Jesus' first disciples, but also to us seeking to follow Jesus today in music and worship ministry. We probably didn't count on things getting this heavy when we signed up for the worship band! And yet, in one of his great upside-down statements, Jesus explains that this is not about depressed, self-hating misery, but quite the contrary. If anyone wants to keep life for themselves, they will lose it; *but*, Jesus says, if you give up your life for me, you will find true life. *The Message* paraphrases it like this:

> Self-help is no help at all. Self-sacrifice is the way, my way, to finding yourself, your true self. What good would it do to get everything you want and lose you, the real you? *(Luke 9:24–25 MSG)*

Following Jesus and leading worship like Jesus must be about self-sacrifice, choosing others before ourselves, letting go of our own preferences. When we do so, we might be surprised

---

77   Leon Morris, *Tyndale New Testament Commentaries: Luke* (IVP, 1999) page 186.

to discover our true potential in Christ and the future God has for us.

Sam has been part of the Resound Worship songwriting group for more than a decade.[78] We started with the principle that all the songs needed to be born in the local church context, but should then be critiqued by the group when we met together and via an online forum. We have experienced many tough lessons in humility as we've put our songs (our babies!) out there for others to question the music, the theology and the poetry. Often we have had to lay down selfish attitudes and personal preferences in order to serve the church better. But it has also been a great joy, as the improved songs have been recorded and shared, and we've heard stories back of how they have blessed individuals and churches. The more we have been able to humble ourselves in the process, the more we have seen God use the songs all over the world. We have been glad that we laid down our original preferences to allow the songs to serve a wider constituency.

DENYING SELF IN WORSHIP MINISTRY

What are the implications of 'denying ourselves' in the context of church worship? Consider for a moment your motives and actions. Are we quicker to be at the front leading, rather than serving in other ways, such as filing the music, putting out the chairs or tidying up the PA? Or how about if we are asked to play with musicians who are at an early stage of their development - are we prepared to risk looking foolish as they make the mistakes it takes to learn and grow?

If we are involved in choosing songs for worship, we need to consider what motivates our decisions. It is tempting to major on our favourites, the songs that make the band or our own voices sound good. We once heard someone say, 'If I was in a secular band, I would choose the songs I liked to play, not what my audience wanted to hear. Why can't worship be the same?' The answer is simple: if we follow the lead of Jesus, our preferences need to come second in order to serve the congregations we lead.

We've also known people choose or change keys of songs which makes them far too high or low for the majority of people to sing, because this will make their own voice sound good. Again, this is not serving the congregation! A hallmark of those who lead worship with the attitude of Jesus is that they put the needs of others before themselves. The amazing thing is that as we begin to do this, God starts to give us joy and satisfaction in seeing other people released to worship. It begins to dawn on us that it is more blessed to give than receive, and that as we lay down our own preferences we can find true life, true worship.

THE PHARISEE AND THE TAX COLLECTOR

When someone steps up to lead worship, you quickly get an idea of how confident that person is. But even with a seemingly confident person, it's hard to judge what they place their confidence *in*. We considered in the previous chapter this amazing truth: 'We have confidence to enter the Most Holy Place by the blood of Jesus' (Hebrews 10:19). Unfortunately, it is easy to forget that our confidence in entering into worship can come *only* via the blood of Jesus, never from our own acts of righteousness. That is what the Pharisee needed to hear in these verses from a story Jesus told:

> To some who were confident of their own righteousness and looked down on everybody else, Jesus told this parable: 'Two men went up to the temple to pray, one a Pharisee and the other a tax collector. The Pharisee stood up and prayed about himself: "God, I thank you that I am not like other men - robbers, evildoers, adulterers - or even like this tax collector. I fast twice a week and give a tenth of all I get."' *(Luke 18:9–12)*

We might not see it immediately, but this Pharisee was actually going beyond what was expected of him in the law. Fasting was commanded once a year, on the Day of Atonement,[79] not twice a week, as many Pharisees did it. The law asked for a tithe of all crops,[80] but Jesus tells us that Pharisees even tithed their garden herbs.[81] The man in the story is making a huge show of his righteousness rather than considering how he might be guilty of a deeper sin - pride.

Does our worship ever get a bit like this? Sometimes we might think that our efforts - the time we spend in prayer, the excellence of our music, the soundness of our theology - are a

---

79   Leviticus 16:29.
80   Deuteronomy 14:22.
81   Luke 11:42.

means of earning God's favour. Or, at least, we can assume that they set us above others whom we judge as somehow inferior: robbers/evildoers/adulterers/queue jumpers/drummers/[insert your pet abomination here].

Compare this to the attitude of the tax collector. Remember that tax collectors at the time were considered to be collaborators with the ruling authorities, raising revenue for them and creaming off the top whatever excess they liked. They were despised, seen as worse than scum. But this tax collector knows his place before God:

> [He] stood at a distance. He would not even look up to heaven, but beat his breast and said, 'God, have mercy on me, a sinner.' *(18:13)*

He comes in a posture of utter humility. The tax collector does not place his confidence in his own achievements, his acts of worship or his service, but throws himself upon the mercy of God. Jesus goes on to shock his audience, turning their expectations upside down by saying, 'I tell you that this man, rather than the other, went home justified before God. For all those who exalt themselves will be humbled, and those who humble themselves will be exalted' (18:14).

There comes a point in our worship (and maybe it should be the starting point) where we need to assume this kind of position before God - the position of humility, acknowledging that all our good works, all our preparation and rehearsal, all our adherence to laws and rules (or our rejection of perceived rules) is inadequate. As Paul the former Pharisee puts it: all of our self-righteousness is rubbish compared to Christ's righteousness.[82] The Message translates these verses particularly vividly:

> Compared to the high privilege of knowing Christ Jesus as my Master, firsthand, everything I once thought I had going for me is insignificant - dog dung. I've dumped it all in the trash so that I could embrace Christ and be embraced by him. I didn't want some petty, inferior brand of righteousness that comes from keeping a list of rules when I could get the robust kind that comes from trusting Christ - God's righteousness. *(Philippians 3:8-9 MSG)*

We need to come to worship humbly. We need to come in repentance. Is there any time for that in your church services? Is there any period where people can say, 'Lord, have mercy on me?' Below are some ways you could do this in a group setting, but before you lead others, the following worship experience will give you space to say 'Lord, have mercy' for yourself.

⏱ PAUSE TO WORSHIP

The Jesus prayer

The Jesus Prayer is an ancient treasure used often in the Eastern Church, a very simple, repeated plea based on

---

82 Philippians 3:8–9.

three passages from Luke's Gospel: 'Lord Jesus Christ, Son of God, have mercy on me, a sinner.'[83]

If you can, find a quiet place without distractions. You may wish to light a candle, look at an icon of Christ or focus on a picture of a calm nature scene, to keep your eyes from wandering. Then slowly breathe in, quietly saying the first half of the prayer, and breathe out as you say the second part.

Unlike meditation in some other religions, the goal is not to empty your mind but to fill it with nothing but Jesus. The prayer acknowledges our need for forgiveness and repentance, while proclaiming who Jesus is. Repeat the prayer as many times as you like (some Orthodox monks say it hundreds of times per day) and allow God to make himself known to you in the quiet of your heart.

☀ IDEAS TO TRY

Confession

In a church or small group setting, there are three important parts to any time of confession: the opportunity to reflect on our sin, the opportunity to confess that sin, and a proclamation that our sin is forgiven in Christ.

Traditional liturgical prayers offer one way of confessing sin and can have great value for many people. Others will be helped by imaginative, multi-sensory approaches

---

83   Luke 17:13; 18:13, 38.

towards confession. Here are some creative suggestions for helping people grasp what forgiveness means.[84]

Write confessions down on paper, then nail the paper to a simple wooden cross. The sound of hammer and nails echoing through a church hall can be spine-tingling. Forgiveness could be proclaimed through pieces of paper printed with a verse such as Psalm 103:12 or 1 John 1:9, which people could take away with them.

Reflect on sin by holding a dirt-covered stone in your hands, then place it in a bucket of water to wash it. Somebody could read out Psalm 51 (or have it printed for people to read) as this happens. Take the clean stone away as a reminder of forgiveness.

Write a confession on 'flash paper', then put it in a metal tin and drop a match on it. The paper immediately burns up, safely and without smoke.

Watch the crucifixion scene from a film of Jesus' life, or a series of still images of the cross, and a version of the *Agnus Dei* (Lamb of God) as a soundtrack.[85] Afterwards, have a time of silence for people to confess their sin, before saying the following prayer together (based on John 1:29): 'Jesus, the Lamb of God, who takes away the sins of the world, washes you clean of all sin.'

---

84   For a host of other creative and multi-sensory ideas visit engageworship.org/confession

85   For example, search iTunes, Spotify or other music stores for settings of the *Agnus Dei* by Rufus Wainwright or Samuel Barber.

You could also use a song expressing the ancient prayer *Kyrie eleison* - Greek for 'Lord, have mercy'.[86] For churches who don't normally engage in corporate confession this can be a helpful place to start. Our favourite setting of the text is by Dinah Reindorf from Ghana, which works well sung *a cappella*.[87]

PETER'S HUMBLE START

Jesus' disciples can be a great comfort to us: they sometimes get things right, but often they mess up spectacularly. We can certainly relate to that in our experiences of leading worship!

Let's start with the disciples getting it right: take a look at Luke 5:1–11. Peter is more than happy to let Jesus use his boat as an impromptu stage for a spot of lakeside preaching. Then, once the teaching is over (or, at least, the spoken part of it), Jesus asks something more unusual of him. Jesus gets involved with the disciples' passion, their craft, and encourages them to take a step of faith with him. He invites them to push the boat out (both literally and metaphorically), to see faith in action by trying for one last catch of fish.

Of course, Peter might respond with pride and unbelief: 'I'm the fisherman here; we've been fishing all night. What would a carpenter or rabbi know about it?' But he doesn't. In humility, he trusts and obeys Jesus. And when we do that, like

---

86   For example: Andy Piercy's 'Father Hear Our Prayer', Geraldine Latty's 'Lord You Hear the Cry', and Joel Payne's 'We Come to You in Sorrow', all available via https://engageworship.org/HWJlinks
87   https://engageworship.org/HWJlinks

Peter, we begin to see miraculous things happen. In his case, it's a catch of fish so big that the boat begins to sink.

Once again, Peter's response is the right one. Like the prophet Isaiah many years before,[88] he falls to his knees in the presence of such holiness and power, saying, 'Go away from me, Lord; I am a sinful man!' (Luke 5:8). He knows that he is entirely unworthy to be with Jesus, to be used by him in such a way. Have you ever reached a moment like that? Do we come to worship with that kind of attitude - that we are unworthy, incapable, on our knees?

We have already discussed some worship ideas that might help a congregation to reach that point. If we do lead people down this path, however, we must also make sure we move on to the next step in the story: the proclamation of our worthiness, not in our own efforts but in Jesus' action to make us so. Like the angel touching Isaiah's lips with the coal, Jesus reassures Peter that he need not be afraid, that he has chosen him as one who will 'catch men and women' (Luke 5:10). We should always leave our congregations with the overriding good news - that Jesus loves them and makes them clean and worthy to stand in his presence.

THE GREATEST - OR THE LEAST?

The disciples start with the right attitude but it is not long before their motives sour.[89] Despite the fact that Jesus restates

---

88   See Isaiah 6:1-8
89   Luke 9:46-55.

his commitment to the road of self sacrifice in verse 44, Luke records three self-centred episodes from the disciples in a row:

> An argument started among the disciples as to which of them would be the greatest. *(Luke 9:46)*

The image of grown men bickering over who is the greatest seems rather comical, and yet, if we are honest, we have probably all had similar conversations. For instance, when speaking to other church leaders, do we drop in comments about how many people have been attending our services recently - just so that they know? Or do we casually mention the name of some famous worship leader we have met? Worse, do we spiritualise our boasting: 'God has blessed us with some great worship times recently'?

The disciples' sin here is pride; in the kingdom of God, there is no ranking in terms of status. Jesus explains that those who consider themselves least are 'great'[90] in the kingdom of heaven. To illustrate his point, he brings out a little child. In Jesus' time children were considered some of the least of all: they were weak, dependent and unimportant. Yet Jesus said that if the disciples welcomed these lowly ones, they welcomed not only him but also the one who sent him, God the Father.

WELCOME FOR THOSE WHO ARE NOT 'ONE OF US'

We need to think through the implications of this teaching for the way we lead worship. Are there people we neglect to 'welcome' in our worship services? How much do you think

---

90   Luke 9:48. Not 'greatest' in the Greek - Morris, *Luke*, page 193.

about the needs of children, or those who are elderly?[91] Are people with special educational needs or disabilities included in our worship?[92] How would someone from another culture, someone who struggles with English, a refugee or asylum seeker engage with your worship?[93] And what about those who are not yet Christian: are your worship practices and language accessible for visitors and seekers? Jesus would challenge us to welcome the minorities and include them - to make the 'least' actually the most important.

It is clear from our passage in Luke that this notion is fairly alien to the disciples, and John tries to clarify the position, thereby scoring the second own goal of the day: "'Master,' said John, "we saw a man driving out demons in your name and we tried to stop him, because he is not one of us"' (9:49).

John thinks that they, as the disciples who travel around with Jesus, have cornered the market on using Jesus' name. Essentially, their sin here is selfishness, wanting to keep Jesus for themselves and denying access to him for others.

To what extent do we do this? Think about churches or groups that worship differently from the way you think is 'correct'. Are you tempted to bad-mouth them in front of

---

91   For help with All Age worship see http://worshipforeveryone.com and our article here - https://www.engageworship.org/all-age-worship
There are a number of resources on worship with the elderly on the Sarum College website, access via https://engageworship.org/HWJlinks

92   A general article on disability and worship from the Calvin Institute can be found via https://engageworship.org/HWJlinks
Two books worth looking at are Kate Tupling, Anna de Lange, *Worship and Disability* (Grove, 2018) and Tony Phelps-Jones *Making Church Accessible to All* (BRF, 2013).

93   This Christian Concern For One World page has a whole host of links for worship with refugees, via https://engageworship.org/HWJlinks

others? Do you resent their success? Sometimes we might even doubt that they can really connect with God, because they are not part of our 'holy club'. Now, we are right to test theology and practice against the Bible; it is not wrong to engage our critical faculties. But Luke shows that we should be careful about passing judgment over other people's ministries, and especially cautious about how we communicate that judgment to others.

FIRE FROM HEAVEN AND OTHER OVERREACTIONS

The disciples' third mistake is simply laughable. James and John (nicknamed 'Sons of Thunder' by Jesus in Mark 3:17) decide that some Samaritans should be punished for not welcoming Jesus. They may have been remembering the story where Elijah calls down fire from heaven upon two captains and their 50 men, because the king had been consulting other gods.[94] So the Sons of Thunder storm up to Jesus and say, 'Lord, do you want us to call fire down from heaven to destroy them?' (Luke 9:54).

This seems like quite an overreaction on their part, and it's a response that goes completely against the heart of Jesus. Once again, they have failed to grasp the sort of Messiah Jesus is - not a bullying military ruler taking the world by force, but a humble servant.

How do you respond to people who are rude to you, those who criticise your playing or your song choices? What about church members who reject your worship style or your

---

94 2 Kings 1:10–12.

point of view? Do people ever get a 'fiery thunderbolt' of words from you, a burning look or a ticking time-bomb of passive aggression?

BE LIKE THE ONE WHO SERVES

The disciples never quite grasped Jesus' true nature during his earthly life. They just could not understand the upside-down nature of his kingdom. Remarkably, even at the Last Supper, Luke records another argument about who is the greatest.

We know from John's Gospel that Jesus then demonstrated his point by getting down on his hands and knees to do the most menial act of service: washing his disciples' feet.[95] And even that act of humble service was not as great as his final one, when he submitted himself to death on a cross, for their sins and for ours.

It's the combination of Jesus' death and resurrection with the coming of the Holy Spirit - to illuminate and enable the disciples - that helps them finally grasp Jesus' kingdom principles. By his blood and his Spirit, the disciples are transformed into humble, serving people, who have the power to heal,[96] the compassion to provide for the needy[97] and the acceptance to release others into ministry and service.[98]

We may feel like failures when it comes to having humility in our lives and ministries. But we should take heart that, just

---

95 John 13:1-17.
96 Acts 3:6.
97 Acts 4:34.
98 Acts 6:3.

as the disciples could be changed by encountering the crucified Jesus and the empowering touch of his Spirit, so can we.

AT LEAST CARE FOR THE LEAST

In Luke's Gospel, Jesus begins his ministry with a powerful manifesto about who he is and what he has come to achieve.

> He went to Nazareth, where he had been brought up, and on the Sabbath day he went into the synagogue, as was his custom. And he stood up to read. The scroll of the prophet Isaiah was handed to him. Unrolling it, he found the place where it is written: 'The Spirit of the Lord is on me, because he has anointed me to preach good news to the poor. He has sent me to proclaim freedom for the prisoners and recovery of sight for the blind, to release the oppressed, to proclaim the year of the Lord's favour.' *(Luke 4:16–19)*

'He's so anointed.' We may have heard that phrase used in church settings to imply that someone is specially gifted, has a kind of hotline to God, perhaps in relation to the way they lead worship. Yet here we see Jesus applying it to himself, not in the context of church leadership but to show that he is set apart to serve and transform the lives of the poor, the marginalised and the outcast. Here the empowering of the Spirit is not for an individualised elevation, but for the sake of others, for the sake of the least.

Jesus' life of perfect worship to the Father is not only to do with spiritual matters. It's not only about blessing Israel

or the important people in society. It's a mission of words
and action, proclamation and demonstration. He preaches
and lives out good news to the poor, the sick, the lonely. In
fact, much of Luke's Gospel is intent on demonstrating Jesus'
bias towards the unlovable.[99] In the rush to improve our sung
worship, our corporate services, have we missed our calling to
worship God by serving the least?

SERVICE AS WORSHIP

One church we were part of felt God's challenge to make
a difference for our local community in acts of service and
blessing. We talked about doing something on a Saturday
or a week night, but agreed that people were already very
busy and we wouldn't be able to guarantee as good a turn-
out as we wanted. So we set aside a whole Sunday (we knew
most people would be available as they would normally be at
church) and planned projects like renovating a single mum's
council flat, redecorating a local school and painting a run-
down community hall.

We were very careful in our wording when promoting
the events. We did not say, 'Next week we are cancelling the
services to do some acts of kindness.' Instead we announced,

---

99   Jesus accepted children (Luke 9:48; 18:16) and women (8:1–3), neither group
having much standing in that culture. He accepted the embarrassing people,
such as a blind man shouting at him, whom others told to shut up (18:35–43). He
accepted 'sinners': Zacchaeus, a despised tax collector (19:1–10), a 'sinful woman'
at the home of a prominent Pharisee (7:36– 50), and other 'outcasts' (15:1–2). He
showed compassion to a demon-possessed man (8:26–39), he risked becoming
ceremonially unclean by touching the dead (7:11–17), he allowed sick people to
touch him (8:43–48) and broke the sabbath rules because of his concern to heal
(13:10–17).

'Next week we are taking our worship outside the walls of this building and glorifying God through serving others.' Painting, cleaning and other activities were transformed from mundane tasks into acts of worship. We took seriously the challenge of Colossians 3:23–24:

> Whatever you do, work at it with all your heart, as working for the Lord, not for human masters, since you know that you will receive an inheritance from the Lord as a reward. It is the Lord Christ you are serving.

Many other churches are also taking seriously the call to service as worship. As a musical worship team, you ought to be leading the way when your congregation decides to bless its community or address a global justice issue, rather than waiting around until the church has 'got over' its social action urge and come back to 'worship'!

We should also consider whether our everyday lives - our relationships, our actions at work, our consumer choices and financial decisions - are honouring the God of justice? Otherwise, at what point does our music become just noise to God, clashing with our lack of concern and action for fairness, the poor and the lonely?[100] The prophet Amos warns us that God may say, 'Away with the noise of your songs! I will not listen to the music of your harps. But let justice roll on like a river, righteousness like a never-failing stream!'

---

100 For more on gathered worship and justice, see Nicholas Wolterstorff, 'Justice as a Condition of Authentic Liturgy', *Theology Today*, vol. 48, no. 1 (1991), pages 6–21.

(Amos 5:23–24). Andy Flannagan has suggested a provocative contemporary paraphrase for these verses:

> I hate your festivals. I cannot stand your worship events. Even though there are thousands of people, and the PA could cause an earthquake, I will not accept them. Even though the band is fantastic, and you have the best worship leader in the world, I have no regard for them. Do you think I care who sells most CDs? Do you think I care what the cool new song is? Away with this individualised, feel-good soundtrack of 'worship'. I'm listening to another channel. It's called Justice and Righteousness, and its arriving on a broadband connection that is wider than you can ever imagine. That's what I want to hear. I know when someone's playing MY song.[101]

💡 IDEAS TO TRY

Connecting with justice

In our book *Whole Life Worship* we have explored three dimensions of worship: the vertical (to God), the horizontal (towards each other) and a third dimension of engagement with the wider world.[102] It may be that we are least well equipped to worship in the light of that third dimension.

---

101 Printed in Spring Harvest Praise 08/09. For more stuff from Andy visit www.andyflan.com

102 Sam and Sara Hargreaves, *Whole Life Worship*, (IVP, 2017), chapter 4.

Here are some suggestions for engaging congregations in lament, intercession and other justice-infused worship. Consider how you could adapt these for your context, or explore other ideas which spring from your tradition.

• **War Sound Effects**: During the civil war in Sri Lanka, our church received an email from some friends there to say that they were worshipping with the sound of gunfire outside their doors. We reflected on the horror of this, and how comfortable our worship in the West can be. Our friend Damian went one stage further, putting together a mix of sound effects which he played into a quiet time of worship. Hearing gunfire, helicopters and babies crying as you sing the Taizé chant 'O Lord, Hear My Prayer' transforms the experience. Praying is no longer a 'head' response - you feel in your gut a compulsion to pray and call out to God for those experiencing conflict.[103]

• **Worship and Justice Confession**: This prayer came out of a conversation with Jo Herbert-James from Tearfund, where we were wrestling with the disconnect between contemporary worship and God's heart for justice. The prayer confesses times when our worship has not been good news to the poor, and asks for God's help to live integrated lives of worship and justice.[104]

• **Dehumanised People**: We were once putting together a worship time focussing on Psalm 139 and Genesis 1:27, thinking about every person being created in God's

103 Download from https://engageworship.org/war-sound Be aware that this could be triggering for those who are particularly nervous or who have experienced conflict themselves.
104 https://engageworship.org/justice-confession

image. We wanted to lament and pray for situations where people had not been treated as 'the image of God', where they had been de-humanised. Our friend Richard put a selection of images together, and our musicians improvised a discordant lament over the top of them. You could do something similar, or play a recorded piece of music, or simply have silence to reflect and pray.[105]

• **Refugee Songs**: Resound Worship has produced two songs which work very well to focus on and intercede for issues around refugees and asylum seekers: Ben Atkins' 'You Are a Refuge'[106] and Joel Payne's 'Our God Was a Refugee'.[107] Bob Hartman's poetic version of Psalm 71 helps us to relate our own situations to those of a refugee.[108]

As our churches look outwards, seeking to respond to the needs of our communities and the wider world, let us ensure that our times of worship are not just inward-looking but also reflect the heart of God for a hurting world.

HUMBLE LIKE JESUS

The potential pitfall when we talk about humility is that some of us can interpret this in a negative way. Self-hatred can be as insidious as pride - to believe that you are worthless or hopeless

---

105 https://engageworship.org/dehumanised
106 https//engageworship.org/refuge
107 https://engageworship.org/HWJlinks
108 https://engageworship.org/refugee-poem

is a lie and a distortion of God's feelings towards you. God is your perfect parent who loves you unconditionally. Jesus gave everything to be with you. You are unique, gifted and beloved. This is the right foundation to base our humility on.

John 13 says this:

> Jesus knew that the Father had put all things under his power, and that he had come from God and was returning to God...

This is a remarkable passage. Jesus was entirely aware of who he was, how powerful he was, where he had come from and where he was going. But this self-knowledge didn't lead to pride. In fact, it inspired the exact opposite response. Look at the very next thing John writes:

> ... so he got up from the meal, took off his outer clothing, and wrapped a towel around his waist. After that, he poured water into a basin and began to wash his disciples' feet, drying them with the towel that was wrapped around him. *(John 13:3-5)*

Jesus was so secure in who he was, where he had come from and where he was going, that he could serve in the most menial way. He could be on his hands and knees, getting his hands dirty, ignoring social stigma. Let's be so secure in who we are in God that we can serve in worship leading with Jesus' sense of rooted selflessness.

CHAPTER 4

LEADER WITH AUTHORITY

We saw in the last chapter that Jesus was the ultimate humble servant. At the same time, it is clear that he was not afraid to give specific instructions to his disciples:

> 'Put out into deep water and let down the nets.'
> 'Tell the people to sit on the ground in groups of fifty.'
> 'Find the donkey that has never been ridden and bring it here.' *(Luke 5:4; 9:14; 19:30)*

Jesus knew where he was heading, and he had the trust of his followers to direct them in that way.

Giving direction within gathered worship can be a challenge. In some churches it is common for the worship team to move from song to song without any spoken words or directions. With their eyes closed and their heads down (or occasionally up towards the ceiling), some worship leaders seem hardly aware of the congregation at all.

The reasoning behind this kind of approach is often based on the humility we explored in the previous chapter, aiming to deflect attention away from the leader and on to God. It is motivated by good intentions. However, the overall effect can be that congregations are unsure of where things are heading. We can get the impression that the leader is so wrapped up in their own worship that the rest of us might as well not be there. They may be worshipping, but they are not *leading*.

The truth is, people like to be led. It can be uncomfortable to be part of a worship time headed up by someone who seems to lack confidence, a sense of direction, or who appears self-absorbed. We should remember that at church we gather for *corporate* worship: we are supposed to be coming to God *together*, offering a unified expression of praise, prayer, response and so on. And that takes some leading.

TOUR GUIDES

Imagine that you are in a new city, let's say York, and you decide to go on a double-decker bus tour to see the delights of the place. You jump on and the driver smoothly guides the bus into the traffic. They begin the tour with a brief, warm welcome and an introduction to the sites you are going to see. Each new landmark is introduced with a few well chosen facts, drawing your attention to items of significant interest, but a lot of the time the driver lets the buildings and the streets speak for themselves. They don't try and pack too much in, but after a forty minute tour you really feel like you've had an encounter with the city.

The next week you're in Bristol, so you decide to do the same thing. Except this time the experience is totally different. The driver lurches away, garbles hello, and then launches in to a string of tired jokes to try and warm you up. They rush from site to site, talking almost all of the time and giving you no time to take in the city for yourself. When you get off the bus you feel shaken by the driving, overwhelmed by the talking and dissatisfied with your experience of touring Bristol.

One analogy for leading worship is to say that we're a bit like tour guides. If we say nothing, give no directions or invitations at all, we fail to lead our congregations. On the other hand, if we act like the second tour guide in our example, filling every moment with our own thoughts and drawing attention to ourselves, we will not leave space for the congregation to have a real encounter with God. People may well leave the service feeling exhausted and confused.

There are helpful times and ways to give verbal instructions to a congregation. Nobody wants a worship leader to rival the preacher in speaking time or theological complexity. Nor is our role to order or nag people ('I want to see more hands in the air!'). Instead, we should see ourselves as permission-givers or facilitators, opening up spaces for people to respond to God.

Have you considered giving instructions as you are leading worship? These can be very simple, for example:

- An invitation to sit, stand, or kneel, or some other physical movement.

- Reading a short Bible passage that fits the flow of worship.
- An encouragement for people to sing out their own spontaneous songs or call out short praise prayers.
- Permission to pause and consider the blessings of the past week.
- An invitation to pray for a situation, silently or out loud.
- A reminder of some attribute of God, and the suggestion that people consider this as they sing the next song or listen to an instrumental section.

These directions are illustrations of how clear leadership can help a congregation go deeper with God in gathered worship. However, they don't cover the breadth of what it means to lead, because they focus only on verbal leadership.

LEADING BEYOND SPEAKING

The words we say to the congregation are not all there is to communication. We might encourage the congregation to 'sing joyfully to God', but if all the worship team members look bored or disengaged it's likely that those non-verbal cues will speak much louder. Jesus' disciples and followers did not just listen to his teaching but imitated his way of living,[109] and Paul tells his readers 'Follow my example, as I follow the example of Christ' (1 Corinthians 11:1).

---

109 John 13:14-15.

Some of you reading this do not have the kind of role where you lead with a microphone. You might be the drummer, or the PA operator, or the organist. You might not attend planning meetings or have an important sounding title - but that doesn't mean you are not a leader. Leadership expert John Maxwell writes:

> The true meaning of leadership is influence - nothing more, nothing less.[110]

Whatever official role you have, however elevated or visible you feel, being part of the worship team means you have a position of influence. The way you play, the facial expressions you show, the attitudes you project and a thousand other tiny things influence members of the congregation. Your musicianship can guide the congregation into a deeper encounter with a text. Your commitment can encourage others to more faithful service. Your enthusiasm to engage with God, the congregation and the world can spark responses from those who see something of Jesus in you. You influence people, and that makes you a leader in the church.

JESUS THE LEADER

Jesus talks a lot about leadership. In Luke 11:37–54 he criticises the religious leaders of the day, listing six 'woes' - ways in which they miss the point, mislead the people and turn the judgment of God upon themselves. He also tells parables about people

---

110 John C Maxwell, *The 21 Irrefutable Laws of Leadership* (Thomas Nelson, 2007) page 16.

who are given leadership responsibility but misuse it. Take the story of the rich man who made one of his servants a leader in charge over the others, to look after them, providing food and care.[111] If the servant had been faithful, he would have been rewarded with even more authority over the rich man's possessions. But when the servant is selfish and negligent, the consequences are dire.

The good news is that because Jesus takes leadership so seriously, he models for us how it should be done and empowers us to do the same. Like the rich man in the story, he will often begin by giving us a small amount of responsibility. Then, as we prove ourselves faithful in it, our spheres of influence increase. Jesus makes the following statement in relation to money, but it can just as easily be applied to leadership:

> 'Whoever can be trusted with very little can also be trusted with much.' *(Luke 16:10)*

It's worth considering what God has entrusted to you and your attitude towards those gifts. Are you investing in the skills and the opportunities to lead that God has given to you? Take a moment to reflect on the authority you have been given and how you exercise that gift.

JESUS AND THE NOTION OF AUTHORITY

For some people, the word 'authority' has very negative connotations. It may remind them of an overbearing parent or an abusive teacher, a fear of the police or other government

---

111 Luke 12:42–48.

institutions. Our society is nervous of control and coercion. So when we lead worship, do we consider ourselves to be under authority or to hold any position of authority ourselves?

Luke's Gospel shows Jesus as one who was described as both coming *under* and *holding* authority. In Luke 4:32 and 36, we read that people were amazed by Jesus' authoritative teaching. Mark's gospel adds the explanation that he did not teach '...as the teachers of the law' (1:22). It wasn't common for rabbis of Jesus' time to teach anything new or original; rather, they offered a mixture of quotes and references. In contrast to them, Jesus spoke as one whose words had authority of their own, without external justification.

Luke also records how Jesus commanded a demon to come out of a man, and the people responded:

> 'With authority and power he gives orders to evil spirits and they come out!' *(Luke 4:36)*

Jesus' authority was not limited to words or to the physical realm. He exercised authority in the spiritual realm, a level of reality beyond what we can normally see but which Luke describes as being very real, having an impact on everyday life. Jesus also describes himself as having authority to forgive sin[112] and acts with authority to drive the merchants out of the temple.[113]

---

112 Luke 5:21–26.
113 Luke 19:45–46.

Having said this, there are moments when Jesus appears to criticise those who exercise authority in an abusive way. For example, at the Last Supper he says:

> 'The kings of the Gentiles lord it over them; and those who exercise authority over them call themselves Benefactors. But you are not to be like that.'
> *(Luke 22:25-26)*

So how are we to understand this concept of authority, and what relevance does it have for us today, especially if we are involved in leading worship? A key may lie in one of Jesus' encounters with a Gentile centurion.

THE CENTURION'S FAITH

The centurion in Luke 7:1–10 is not ethnically Jewish but he is well loved by the locals for building them a synagogue, so the community leaders take a message from him to Jesus, asking him to come and heal the centurion's sick servant. As Jesus is on his way, a second group of the centurion's friends turn up with a rather strange message:

> 'Lord, don't trouble yourself, for I do not deserve to have you come under my roof. That is why I did not even consider myself worthy to come to you. But say the word, and my servant will be healed. For I myself am a man under authority, with soldiers under me. I tell this one, "Go," and he goes; and that one, "Come,"

and he comes. I say to my servant, "Do this," and he does it.' *(Luke 7:6–8)*

At this point, something happens that never happens at any other point in the Gospels: Jesus *marvels* at someone. He is amazed, blown away. Far from thinking that this is a stupid idea, he praises the centurion for his great faith - greater than he has found in all Israel.

The centurion understands the nature of Jesus' authority. He himself is under the authority of his higher-ranking commanders and he has people under his authority. He knows that, in the spiritual realm, Jesus is under the authority of God the Father and has authority over lesser spiritual beings - angels, demons and so on. He knows that you cannot have one without the other: you must be under authority to be able to exercise authority over someone else.

Jesus himself confirms this understanding in Luke 10:17–22. At this point, Jesus is 'full of joy' because the disciples have come back and reported that demons obeyed them in Jesus' name. He explains to them that 'my Father has given me authority over everything' (v. 22, NLT), and that he has passed this authority on to them so that they can have power over the enemy. He is both under the authority of the Father and able to delegate authority to those under him.

AUTHORITY BASED ON LOVE

It is important to realise that this kind of authority is not the same as a dictatorial, manipulative power-trip. Right here in Luke 10 Jesus uses the Greek word corresponding to the Aramaic *Abba*, the childlike name similar to our 'Daddy', an intimate term of loving devotion used uniquely at this time by Jesus to address the Father.[114] Human sinfulness has twisted 'authority' into a selfish and damaging concept but, at its heart, true authority reflects the perfect relationships of the Trinity: the Father being served by the Son and the Spirit in reciprocal, mutual love.[115]

It is vital to understand this in relation to the way we lead worship. If Jesus himself was both under authority and exercised it over people and the spiritual realm, so must we. We cannot expect to have authority unless we submit ourselves to it, and yet we also cannot think of ourselves as leaders of worship without considering the authority and responsibility we have been given over others.

Firstly and most importantly, we are under the authority of God. As Jesus passed authority on to his disciples to heal the sick, cast out demons[116] and take the message of repentance to all the nations,[117] so he also passes it on to us. As followers of Christ, we are under the authority of God and he gives us authority in the spiritual and earthly realms to do his will. If God has called you to lead or be involved in worship, in whatever context or medium, he has given you the authority to do so. We do not need to prove ourselves or invent any other earthly credentials.

---

114 Marshall, *Luke*, page 433.
115 See also John 5:19-20.
116 Luke 9:1.
117 Luke 24:47.

RELATING TO HUMAN LEADERSHIP

We are under the authority of God, and yet God has also set up the earthly structures of authority to be a protection and a blessing to us. Paul says to the Romans:

> Let everyone be subject to the governing authorities, for there is no authority except that which God has established. The authorities that exist have been established by God. Consequently, whoever rebels against the authority is rebelling against what God has instituted, and those who do so will bring judgment on themselves. *(Romans 13:1–2)*

The writer to the Hebrews also tells us:

> Have confidence in your leaders and submit to their authority, because they keep watch over you as those who must give an account. Do this so that their work will be a joy, not a burden, for that would be of no benefit to you. *(Hebrews 13:17)*

This means that, in a church context, we are to submit to those who lead us: pastors, vicars, elders, churchwardens, paid church staff - whatever kind of authority structure is set up. Sometimes we might disagree with them, and it is not wrong to question or discuss, so long as we do it with the right attitude of humility and grace. However, at the end of the day, we are to respect their position as given by God and trust that God will hold them to account for their responsibilities[118].

In our experience, as we have honoured our leadership in listening to their advice and instruction, it has been very releasing. It is a great safety net to be able to exchange meaningful looks or a few words with our pastors and service leaders while we have been leading worship, and in a wider sense to come under their guidance and authority.

In very practical terms, consider your relationship with those in authority over you. The way you think and talk about your leaders - your attitude towards them - will determine your relationship with them. Relating well to leaders can look as simple as getting in touch with pastors and preachers before planning a service, making sure we find out themes and their angle on things. It also involves honouring the wishes of your leaders as you lead worship, rather than pushing boundaries or trying to lead the congregation in different directions to the vision of the church.

It is easy to feel that once we are behind a microphone we have power. Yet that power must be submitted first to God and second to the leaders who are appointed over us. Only then comes the right to exercise the authority we have over others, with the added responsibility of leading well.

---

118   Having said all this, sadly there are examples of abusive, manipulative or even illegal behaviour in church leadership. In these circumstances we must speak up to protect the vulnerable and feel free to walk away from an unhealthy situation. Your leaders not being accountable to a further level of authority is a warning sign.

① PAUSE TO WORSHIP

Leaders

God is gracious in providing people in authority over us, to lead and inspire us. Spend a moment thinking about this and listening to God. Who are the people that God has sent into your life for this purpose, now or in the past? How have they encouraged, challenged and protected you? Is there anyone with whom that relationship has been difficult?

Give thanks to God for these people, mentioning them by name before him and asking him to bless them. If the relationships have been more challenging, you may wish to hand over how you feel to God, or ask for his forgiveness.

Write a letter or card to one of these people, thanking them for taking leadership seriously, and naming some specific things about their ministry that have blessed and encouraged you. (If you're going to do it, do it now, before you forget!)

KNOW WHERE YOU ARE HEADING

In the early 2000's when we were first married, travelling though London required planning. We would get out our trusty A-Z and our tube map and carefully plot the best route to our destination. Then came smart phones and Google maps, and all of a sudden we stopped planning our journeys and started blindly following the dot on the screen. The weakness of this approach becomes very real in those frightening moments when the battery runs out, or the phone loses signal. You will probably know that particular cold fear of not knowing where you're going.

Jesus was clear about where he was going. He knew the road to his destination: that he was sent to proclaim the kingdom in word and deed,[119] and that his work as the Messiah was to be brought to completion through suffering, death and resurrection.[120] His dramatic meeting with Moses and Elijah on the mount of transfiguration[121] seems to have clarified things for him further: 'They spoke about his departure, which he was about to bring to fulfilment at Jerusalem' (Luke 9:31).

From this point on, Jesus 'set his face' towards Jerusalem,[122] knowing that this city was the place where he must complete his mission. When some Pharisees tried to warn him that Herod wanted his blood, he was unshakeable in his resolve:

> He replied, 'Go tell that fox, "I will drive out demons and heal people today and tomorrow, and on the third day I will reach my goal." In any case, I must keep going today and tomorrow and the next day - for surely no prophet can die outside Jerusalem!' *(Luke 13:32–33)*

As leaders, it's very important for us to follow Jesus' example in seeking God, reflecting on his word and listening to the

---

119 Luke 4:18-19.
120 Luke 9:22.
121 Luke 9:28-36.
122 Luke 9:51 NRSV.

people he sends our way in order that we might know direction for our ministry. This applies to the big picture: how we want worship in our church to develop over the next few years, the goals we want to achieve as a team, the values and ethos we want to permeate every act of worship in our church. If you lead a worship team, we would encourage you to take time and work through these issues with your group.

LEADERSHIP AND SERVICE PLANNING

Knowing where we're going also applies in smaller-scale matters, particularly how we go about planning a time of corporate worship. Of course, the Spirit can prompt us to speak or lead in the spur of the moment, but he can also guide us during preparation a few days or even weeks beforehand.

When we (Sam and Sara) are preparing for a time of corporate worship, we go through something like the process outlined in the bonus section at the end of the book - 'Planning a Journey of Worship'.[123] This encourages us to think of worship as a journey, leading people through a series of different sections or 'functions' of worship, each with a different but interlinked aim. For many worship leaders, their only explicit aim will usually be 'glorifying God' or 'adoring God', and of course that is very important, but these are not the only aims we can have for our worship.

We know that Jesus, as a devout and observant Jewish worshipper, regularly sang the Psalms. To some extent the range of worship expressions found there should be an indication of

123 This is also covered in session 2B of the video course: 'Planning a Worship Journey'.

what we can hope to express in worship. In the Psalms we see worship which includes:

- Gathering people (Psalm 95:1–2)
- Praising God (66:1–4)
- Remembering God's deeds in recent and personal experience (40:1–3), and in our corporate life and long ago (78:1–4; 136:1–26)
- Giving thanks (92:1–4)
- Placing trust in God (25:1–3)
- Recognising God's holiness and majesty (29:1–11; 93:1–5)
- Coming quietly to hear his voice (95:6–7; 131:1–2)
- Contemplating how nature reveals and glorifies God (19:1–6; 104:1–32)
- Intimate adoration (63:1–8)
- Lament, expressing sorrow over disappointment or tragedy (22:1–2; 137:1–4)
- Confession and absolution: personal (51:1–17) and corporate (130:1–8)
- Intercession: for justice (58:1–11), for the world (67:1–7) and for ourselves (80:1-3)
- Reflecting on and responding to God's word (119:9–16)
- Remembering what God thinks of us (139:1–18)
- Pronouncing blessing (121:5–8)

This is obviously not an exhaustive list, but it shows some of the many expressions or functions of worship into which we can lead people. Many of these have been forgotten or neglected by contemporary churches, but it's part of our role as worship leaders to revive them in relevant ways.

Some of these expressions may already happen in your church, but may not fall under the remit of the worship leader. For example, the pastor or service leader might always lead the confession, or a rota of people might lead the intercessions. It's still worth considering how you might help resource these movements of worship, perhaps drawing them into the singing time or expressing them in some other creative way. Indeed, we want to encourage you strongly, wherever possible, to plan worship as a team, with the service leader or preacher and/or with other creative people who can come up with different movements and expressions of worship.

We hope that the structure in the 'Planning a Journey of Worship' section might encourage you to think through the journey of a corporate worship time, and help your song and media choices be more intentional. It has been our experience that when leaders engage with this process, their worship leading begins to have clearer shape and they're able to take the congregation on a journey towards an encounter with God. Have a go and see for yourself!

DEVELOPING A WORSHIP TEAM

Any church which wants to see its worship life grow will need to build a team. Not just a 'group' or a 'band', but a diverse yet unified team, working together for a shared goal, continually developing and passing on leadership.

Jesus was, perhaps, the ultimate team builder. Just look at the results: he took a ragbag bunch of misfits and transformed them into the kind of leadership team that would take his message and his movement to the far corners of the earth. He built a team that defended and proclaimed his story in the face of persecution and death threats, founded a church that helped to transform history and is still growing today worldwide. Something about what he did with those disciples *worked*, and we can learn from it as we think about building teams in our churches.

The first thing we notice is the way Jesus builds relationships with his team. They don't just meet for worship once a week, but constantly travel, live, eat, laugh, bicker and grow together, becoming more like family. Before you start thinking about going to conferences, running music lessons or holding Bible studies, begin with growing the relationships within your worship team. Do things together which will help you go deeper in how you relate, whether that is having meals or drinks together, working on a shared project or taking a day trip.

In one church team we led, we instigated a monthly gathering which included food, worship and testimony. Things were shared in the room which we would never have learned just from meeting to rehearse each week, and we began to know one another on a more profound level. We would be vulnerable and pray for one another, and the group dynamics improved greatly. Growing together in trust, understanding and love will lay the right foundation for any further development.

CHARACTER FIRST

When you consider building a team, you may be wondering how you ought to identify people for worship ministry. We might look for team members with obvious gifts in music or the creative arts, and of course such gifts are important. We might look for spiritual maturity, and that is also good. But when Jesus first calls his disciples, they demonstrate neither gifts nor maturity. It seems that Jesus was looking first for character. We have already discussed in Chapter 3 how he tested Peter's character, giving him simple tasks such as asking to use his boat and instructing him to go out for a final catch of fish. Peter responded with generosity, trust and obedience.[124]

This is very important for us to remember. A great singer, musician or artist may join our church, and we can be very tempted to involve them straight away in upfront worship ministry. Yet what do we know about their character? Do they respond well to instruction and critique? Are they willing to serve, and learn?

Often it's helpful to give potential team members small tasks, to see if they are prepared to help with making the coffee or setting up equipment or filing music. If they are prepared to serve with humility and good humour in the small things, they will most probably be a joy to have in the worship team. If someone wanted to lead worship in our church, we would give them the opportunity to lead in a small prayer meeting or a home group, to see how they acted in this context, and

---

124 Luke 5:1-11.

with what attitude they received feedback and constructive criticism.

Recently, we struggled to find a bass player for an event as none of our usual musicians were available. We took a chance on a young guy who was recommended to us, and we were curious to see whether he would gel with our band. There was one particular moment when we exchanged a look between us saying 'yep, we got the right guy!' That was the moment the young bassist joined in with some ridiculous children's song actions, showing both humility and team spirit. It was a small thing that demonstrated this person's character, and he showed the same attitude for the rest of the project in both small and big tasks.

MENTORING YOUR TEAM

Jesus had a wider band of followers but he also chose a smaller circle of disciples in whom he invested more time. He made this key decision in an attitude of prayer:

> One of those days Jesus went out to a mountainside
> to pray, and spent the night praying to God. When
> morning came, he called his disciples to him and chose
> twelve of them, whom he also designated apostles.
> (Luke 6:12–13)

Prayer and space to listen to God ought to be the foundation of recruiting people to be in your team. This is especially true when you identify a smaller circle of key individuals whom you plan to mentor and develop. We have found that sometimes

God will lead us to invest in less obvious people, those without the flashy gifts or experience, who may prove to be among our most fruitful relationships. We probably would not have discovered such people without first going to God in prayer.[125]

Again, this principle doesn't have to apply just to the main 'team leader'. Every team member could be looking out for one of two people at an earlier stage of ministry to whom they could be passing on their experience and encouragement.

Jesus invested a great amount of time and effort in his key team, the apostles, and even more to his inner circle of Peter, James and John. He spent almost all his time with the disciples, often turning from the crowds to speak just to them,[126] explaining his teaching in greater depth and allowing them to ask questions. We can certainly learn from this as leaders, as it is always worthwhile to create time to go for a coffee or simply chat with key team members.

For us, in the past we have made it a habit to meet with newer worship leaders for up to an hour before worship rehearsals, to talk and pray through the song choices and any other issues that might have come up for them. Make sure you listen to how they feel, and give them space to bring up concerns or questions. Encourage them and pray with them.

It's important to share honest and encouraging feedback about how someone has led a service, so that they can grow from each experience. In these contexts we have found that a 'feedback sandwich' is a pastorally helpful structure:

---

125 We've learned a lot about recruiting in prayer from Mark Yaconelli's book, *Contemplative Youth Ministry* (SPCK, 2006).
126 Luke 10:23-24.

- Start with an area of encouragement. Be as specific as you can - 'I thought it was really helpful when you did this _____.'
- Then bring up one area for improvement. Again, be specific - 'You could think about how you link from the praise songs to the prayer activity', or 'The musical arrangement of that hymn seemed to be working against the words, can you think how you could make them complement one another?', or 'The instrumental passage in that opening song was really long, how could we deal with that?'
- Finally, end with another encouragement - 'I was really drawn into worship when you _____. You are really growing as a worship leader!'

Make sure the people you are mentoring have opportunities to see you minister, and get to be part of the preparation that goes into the services you lead. Jesus began by allowing the disciples to observe him as he ministered.[127] Modelling good practice is essential for any team leader. But don't leave it too long before you let them have a go themselves: only a few chapters into Luke's Gospel, Jesus lets the disciples loose!

THE DISCIPLES' FIRST MISSION

> When Jesus had called the Twelve together, he gave them power and authority to drive out all demons and

---

127 Luke 7:11.

> to cure diseases, and he sent them out to preach the
> kingdom of God and to heal the sick. *(Luke 9:1–2)*

Luke 9 has some important lessons for us about how to release
people into ministry. Jesus entrusts the disciples with the very
same mission that he himself has exercised so far: to preach
the kingdom and heal the sick. He passes his authority and
power on to them. There comes a point when we need to deal
with any control issues we may have and let someone else have
a go at our ministry.

The truth is, Jesus knew that his mission would fail
unless he effectively multiplied himself twelve, 72 and then
thousands of times over. Notice Luke's care in placing the note
about Herod's growing awareness of all that Jesus has done
at this specific point in the story.[128] He wants us to see that,
although Jesus himself is making waves, it's when he sends out
others that people really begin to take notice. This should be
an encouragement to us to train, equip and release others in
ministry.

Jesus does not make it easy for his disciples: he drops
them in the deep end, with instructions that sound almost
ridiculous. Don't take a walking stick, or a bag, or food, or
money, or an extra coat.[129] Did Jesus want them to freeze, or
starve?

Understanding the cultural context really helps here.
Many travelling teachers would make a good living out of
walking (with their recognisable wooden stick) from place to

128 Luke 9:7-9.
129 Luke 9:3.

place, collecting money in their bag in return for dispensing some 'wisdom'. Often they would begin by staying in one of the more modest houses in the village. Then, if what they said pleased people, they would be invited to better and better houses, trading-up as their stay went on.[130]

Jesus is determined that the disciples will bear as little resemblance to these religious salesmen as possible. The gospel is not to be hawked for monetary gain. The disciples are not to trade-up, but to honour the lowly houses whose residents first invite them in. Jesus is showing them how to conduct themselves with values that are different from those of the world around them. We should do the same with our teams, ensuring that the glory of God and the serving of the congregation are their highest goal - not money, or recognition, or any other self-centred aim.

The second reason for these instructions is that the disciples are to do as Jesus has done; trusting God, not earthly possessions, for their provision and care. It is tempting to think in worship ministry that if we just had a slightly better guitar, or a bigger PA, or more professional sounding backing tracks, then our worship would really take off. God often does provide these resources for us, and they are not inherently wrong, yet sometimes we can rely on them and forget to trust in God alone to make worship happen.

Think about what people in your team rely on. It might be the a large music group, or pre-recorded synth pad loops, or the projector screen, or something else. Are there situations

---

130 Marshall, *Luke*, pages 352-353.

where you could encourage your mentees to step away from these bits of scaffolding, even just for one song, and rely more on God than technology or music?

WHEN TEAM BUILDING GOES SOUR

The final aspect of Jesus' team building that we want to highlight is found as part of his conversation during the last supper:

> 'Simon, Simon, Satan has asked to sift you as wheat. But I have prayed for you, Simon, that your faith may not fail. And when you have turned back, strengthen your brothers.' *(Luke 22:31–32)*

Notice here that Jesus is praying for his core team personally. We should make it a habit to pray specifically and regularly for our team members and those we mentor, asking God to speak to us about them, especially about any areas where they may be struggling.

In his times of prayer for Peter, Jesus has heard from the Father that the devil is out to entrap Peter. Peter hotly refutes the idea at the meal, then goes on to deny Jesus three times as the cockerel crows.[131] It is encouraging to know that Jesus still loved Peter even though he knew he was going to let him down, and he still had a central role for Peter to play in his kingdom movement.[132] This should encourage us when we fail, and it points to what our reaction should be when other people hurt

131 Luke 22:54–62.
132 John 21:15–19.

or let us down. In all team and mentoring relationships, there will inevitably be times when we feel rejected or disappointed by the people in whom we invest.

In our ministry in local churches there have been worship team members who we have struggled with. At times they have been difficult to lead, and have caused tensions among the team and with the wider church. On more than one occasion people have sent angry emails blaming us for all kinds of things, and sometimes this has climaxed in them resigning from the team under a cloud of resentment.

If you have been in a similar situation, you will know how devastating that can be. Think about how Jesus would have felt, standing across the courtyard and hearing Peter repeat three times, 'I do not know him' (Luke 22:56–62). Like Jesus, we must be prepared for rejection and disappointment from those we lead. More than that, we need to ask God for his strength to forgive people's mistakes, whether or not they apologise. And we need to rely on God for the grace to reinstate those who genuinely ask for forgiveness and a second chance.

DITCHES, PLANKS, ROTTEN ROOTS AND SHAKY FOUNDATIONS

We have considered leading the congregation and leading a team. Both of these are challenging and serious callings which depend entirely on a third factor: your ability to lead *yourself*. In Luke 6 Jesus tells a bunch of stories about the hazards of failing to lead ourselves well. He talks of one blind man leading another blind man, and both of them ending up in a ditch. Next there's the one about the fellow with a huge plank lodged in his eye, starting to prod around in some other poor guy's face, who only has a speck to deal with.[133]

The stories seem laughable, but are perhaps less funny if you are the blind man trying to lead, or the man with a plank in his eye, whom Jesus calls a 'hypocrite'. Even worse is the situation of those who have to follow these failing leaders, as they are dragged into ditches and wrongly accused.

Jesus continues this passage by speaking about trees with bad roots that don't bear fruit, and houses built on shaky foundations.[134] The point he seems to be making again and again is 'get yourself right before you begin to lead others'. Tree roots and foundations are unseen, yet they have a huge impact on the fruit or the stability of the ministry that rests on them. What is hidden in our hearts will, eventually, begin to overflow out of our mouths. How we lead ourselves in the secret places, behind the closed doors of our homes or in the moments at work when we think nobody sees: this will eventually spill over into how we lead at church. The most important thing you can do for your worship leading is allow God to transform you from the inside out.

---

133 Luke 6:39-42.
134 Luke 6:43-49.

🕐 PAUSE TO WORSHIP

Roots and foundations

Picture a tree, and imagine the soil dug away so the roots are visible. Or picture a house, with the ground exposed so you can see the foundations. Choose one of these images, and imagine you are the tree or the house. What are your roots? What are your foundations?

Take a moment to write down what you see when you look at your roots or your foundations. You may even want to draw this. Think about what is going on under the surface of your life. Are there negative attitudes, selfish ambitions, destructive habits, or other hidden problems? Are your rooted in God, or are there unhelpful things sabotaging your foundations?

Talk to God about these things. If appropriate, say you are sorry and receive God's forgiveness.

Then begin to replace any negative things with positive, truthful, godly things. What do you *want* to be your foundations? What do you want to be filling your heart, so that what you do and say is overflowing from a well of godly attitudes?

Receive God's Spirit afresh to empower you to lead yourself well, so this will overflow into your leadership of others.

CHAPTER 5

CREATIVE COMMUNICATOR

At one point when Jesus is teaching the crowds, he asks:

> 'What is the kingdom of God like? What shall I
> compare it to?' *(Luke 13:18)*

We like to imagine Jesus here staring off into the middle distance, maybe even scratching his beard as he ponders aloud: how can I explain this? What image will bring it to life? How can I communicate in a way that relates to the people around me?

We are told in Matthew that Jesus '...did not say anything to them without using a parable' (13:34). So he must have constantly been asking these kinds of questions: What stories will they grasp? What illustration will show a new angle of what the kingdom of God is like? And in this particular instance, he lands on a tiny, ordinary thing:

'It is like a mustard seed, which a man took and
planted in his garden. It grew and became a tree, and
the birds perched in its branches.' *(Luke 13:19)*

A mustard seed was an everyday object for the rural community
in Galilee at the time. Everyone knew what a mustard seed
looked like, felt like in your hand and tasted like. It's like that
common trope of observational stand-up comedy: 'What's the
deal with aeroplane food... or telemarketing... or IKEA...?'
Comedians will often find something their listener connects
with, and then add a punch line.[135]

In a similar way, Jesus takes this thing that everyone
knows from their ordinary lives, and claims that it's like
the kingdom of God. 'How?' the crowd may well wonder.
Firstly, Jesus explains; it's a tiny thing that grows surprisingly
large. Just like the kingdom of God, it starts small and looks
unimpressive, but will expand beyond our imagination.

But there is a further twist: 'the birds perched in its
branches'. This might seem like just a little throwaway line
to add a pastoral, idyllic flavour to the scene. But actually, it
is surprising and subversive, and may well have infuriated the
Pharisees if spoken plainly. The crowd would have recognised
the term 'All the birds of the air' as an Old Testament image
for all the peoples of the earth.[136] What we end up with is
an image of the kingdom of God being a movement which
arrives small and humbly, not powerfully and triumphantly as

135 For example Jerry Seinfeld's joke: 'What's the deal with lampshades? I mean if
it's a lamp, why do you want shade?'
136 Daniel 4:12, 21; Ezekiel 17:23; 31:6. Morris, *Luke*, page 246.

hoped for by Jesus' contemporaries. Eventually, it will grow large enough to provide a home for all the nations, not just the people of Israel. Jesus' teaching is relatable, memorable, and mind-blowing, and all packed into just two short sentences.

JESUS THE CREATIVE COMMUNICATOR

The preachers and teachers among us could only hope to provide such a powerful message in so few words. But for a moment, let us focus less on what Jesus said and more on how he said it. Jesus was a storyteller, a speaker of parables and proverbs, and a very creative one at that. For example:

- His parables varied depending on his audience: to rich people he spoke of business and finance;[137] to those who thought themselves righteous he told tales of judgment;[138] to large crowds he used familiar farming metaphors.[139]
- He used current events, the news of the day, to teach about the ways of God.[140]
- He developed an idea using a trilogy of images, building his point as in the stories of the lost sheep, the lost coin and, most dramatically, the lost son.[141]

Although storytelling seems to have been Jesus' main approach, he also employed visual aids. When asked, 'Who is

137 Luke 12:13–21.
138 Luke 18:9–14.
139 Luke 8:4–8.
140 Luke 13:1–5.
141 Luke 15.

the greatest?' he drew a young child into the circle - a striking, tangible image of humility.[142] When people tried to trick him with questions about taxes, he asked them to hold up a Roman coin, and the picture of Caesar helped him avoid the trap.[143] Most importantly, he used the everyday physical symbols of bread and wine to initiate the most significant act of Christian worship in history, Holy Communion.[144]

Jesus was clearly a talented storyteller, but to find the root of his creativity we need to remember what we covered in Chapter 2 - the fact that Jesus was fully human. And humans are made to echo the creativity of God.

MADE IN THE IMAGE OF A CREATOR

> Just imagine for a moment, that we were made by a creative God. More than that, imagine that this creative God put his own character into us, because he wanted us to be creative too. Imagine that he longed for us to have a tiny glimpse of the thrill he had when he made the whole world out of nothing. Imagine he put his Spirit inside us to free us, inspire us and enable us to become all we can be.[145]

Genesis 1 tells of God crafting endless diversity and wonder out of nothing. The poem paints a picture of God's delight

---

142 Luke 9:46-48.

143 Luke 20:20-26.

144 Luke 22:17-20.

145 Rob Lacey, *Are We Getting Through?* (Silver Fish, 1999) page 22.

in making all things good. And then at the high point of this story, this creative God:

> … created mankind in his own image, in the image of God he created them; male and female he created them. (*Genesis 1:27*)

If God is creative, and we are made in his image, then part of that image must be that we are creative too. Not creating out of nothing as God does, but echoing God's inventive, playful, surprising, beautiful, truthful, problem-solving, visionary nature in the ways we live, work and worship.

Many people in the church feel that they are not creative. Some have been told from a young age that they 'can't draw', 'can't sing', or that their poetry is worthless doggerel. In church services we can elevate certain art forms - preaching for example, or music - whereas other gifts such as photography, poetry, flower arranging or interior design can be ignored. We give opportunities to those who have confidence or training, but fail to encourage people who are just exploring new forms of expression. It is sadly the case that many gifts go unrecognised, and many people feel discouraged from using their natural, God-given creativity in worship.

Sam was staying for the weekend with some friends who have two young daughters. On the way to the house he bought some pens, sticker books and coloured paper as a gift. He gave these to the the girls as he arrived, and they ran off to play. Imagine his delight when 20 minutes later they returned with the artworks they had created - funny figures, inventive scenes and imaginative landscapes. In this ordinary, slightly messy family moment, Sam sensed God saying: 'This is what I do with all my children. I give gifts, and I don't make any demands on how you use them. But I delight to see every time you take those gifts and make something new.'

Further on in the creation story, God gives Adam the creative task of naming the animals. It says that God brought the animals to the man 'to see what he would name them' (Genesis 2:18). Can you imagine God, your perfect parent, giving you gifts and then looking on with excited anticipation to see what you will do with them? God has that kind of baited-breath expectation over you, over your congregation, and over your church's worship. How will you respond?

JESUS' AND OUR HUMANITY

Jesus fulfils what God intended for us in creation - he is the fullness of what it means to bear God's image.[146] And as such, he engaged with the breadth of his hearers' humanity. He related to them not purely on an intellectual or spiritual level, but connecting with the fullness of their existence. His communication and the ways he drew people in to engage with God included not only creative words, but also opportunities to touch, to taste, to smell and to see. In his first letter, John writes:

> That which was from the beginning, which we have heard, which we have seen with our eyes, which we

---

146 Colossians 1:15.

have looked at and our hands have touched – this we proclaim concerning the Word of life. *(1 John 1:1)*

Look again at all those different senses - John *heard* Jesus, *saw* him, even reached out and *touched* him. The incarnation was a multi-sensory experience. The Word became flesh.[147]

This has remarkable implications for our worship. If Jesus was fully human, and engaged the fullness of his followers' humanity, shouldn't we do the same for our congregations? Some sections of the modern, Western church are in danger of focussing on words more than flesh, intellect more than experience. Worship is diminished to be about saying and singing the right things. In other traditions experience is key, but it is an abstract spiritualised experience which seems to ignore our everyday human experience. In these contexts we might close our eyes and lose ourselves in the moment, but it can have very little impact on our daily reality.

If we are to be inspired by Jesus' way of communicating, it will mean embracing worship which reconnects with our physical humanity. On a very practical note, it might mean considering which of the five senses we are engaging with each time we gather.

---

147 John 1:14. For a deeper look at this see Aidan Nichols, *The Art of God Incarnate: Theology and Image in Christian Tradition* (Darton, Longman and Todd, 1980) and William A Dyrness, *Visual Faith* (Baker Academic, 2001).

💡 IDEAS TO TRY

Using the five senses

• **Taste:** We have used food from around the world in worship to remind people that we are part of a global church. We have also given out spoons of honey and glasses of cold water, encouraging people to reflect on the song lyric 'Your name is like honey on my lips, your Spirit like water to my soul'[148] while actually experiencing those tastes.

• **Touch**: Consider what simple objects you could have people hold or touch to reflect on a prayer theme or Bible passage. For example, we have provided large, rough nails for people to hold as they consider Jesus on the cross. Another idea is to hand out modelling clay and ask people to work it into a shape which represents how they feel before God.[149] We have given out bricks while talking about Nehemiah rebuilding the walls of Jerusalem, inviting people to write their names on them with marker pens.

• **Smell:** You can read Revelation 8:3–4 and talk about our prayers rising as incense to God, while burning some incense sticks or lighting a censer. Perfume can help people consider the woman's extravagant offering of praise in Luke 7:36–50. Encourage the sense of smell by providing fragrant flowers when reflecting on Jesus'

---

148 'Holy and Anointed One' by John Barnett. https://engageworship.org/ HWJlinks

149 There is a variation on this idea here - https://engageworship.org/clay

call for us to 'consider how the wild flowers grow' (Luke 12:27).

• **Sight**: Project appropriate visual art on a screen for people to meditate on, or ask artists in your church to make original pieces to use for reflection. Also be aware of the visuals which you may not ask people to reflect on specifically, but are still visible during worship communicating something - pictures behind song words, banners on the wall, graphics in notice sheets, the way the building is lit, and so on.

• **Hearing**: If you play in a worship band, consider how you can develop your musical arrangements to engage the congregation, and experiment with musical styles outside of your norm to express a wider range of emotions. Beyond music, we have used sound effects to enhance a Bible reading, such as thunder and lightning followed by gentle waves for the calming of the storm,[150] or noises of war and suffering to inspire prayer.[151]

AN EXTRAVAGANT, MULTI-SENSORY OFFERING

Luke 7:36–50 records the actions of a 'sinful' woman, who comes in repentance to Jesus for the life she has been living. Within the culture of the time, her gender would have been reason enough for Jesus to ignore her presence at the table. Her 'reputation' would have made his acknowledgment of her all the more shocking to the other guests. It seems that her

---

150 Luke 8:22-25.

151 https://engageworship.org/war-sound

tearful repentance turns into an act of multi-sensory worship and adoration as she discovers Jesus' loving acceptance. Simon the Pharisee is too busy judging her to see that it is in fact he himself who is sinning - neglecting to provide Jesus with foot-washing and ignoring his own need for forgiveness.

> Then [Jesus] turned toward the woman and said to Simon, 'Do you see this woman? I came into your house. You did not give me any water for my feet, but she wet my feet with her tears and wiped them with her hair. You did not give me a kiss, but this woman, from the time I entered, has not stopped kissing my feet. You did not put oil on my head, but she has poured perfume on my feet. Therefore, I tell you, her many sins have been forgiven - for she loved much. But the one who has been forgiven little loves little.' *(Luke 44–47)*

The woman in the story worshipped Jesus not by singing to him but by offering him the best, most precious thing she had - expensive perfume, worth far more than the oil that Simon could not be bothered to give Jesus. This story should raise questions about our own attitude towards worshipping Jesus. If we are aware of the extent to which we have been forgiven, and the great love Jesus has shown us, do we respond with 'great love' in extravagant offerings of worship? This woman can inspire us to pour out our best for Jesus.

In John's account of a similar story, Judas complains that the money the woman spent on the perfume could have been given to the poor, but John adds that he said this only because he was greedy.[152] Do we ever fall back on the excuse that time, money or effort spent on gathered worship is 'wasteful'?

This is a creative and experiential offering of worship - imagine how intoxicating the smell of the perfume must have been as it filled the room. She also offered her tears, her hair, her hands, her lips - tactile, multi-sensory and intimate expressions of adoration.

SENSES AND SIMPLICITY

Using several of the senses over the space of a worship service helps to engage the whole person and express more of who God is. It affirms our humanity and can release worship in ways that singing or praying alone might not. Sometimes it is appropriate to spend a little extra time and resources to prepare something creative and multi-sensory, perhaps remembering the forgiven woman of Luke 7 as our inspiration.

Often, however, creative worship can be very simple. It does not have to look like a lavish stage show, an expensive multi-media event or a complex art installation. Sometimes removing something can be the creative thing to do: for example, lighting a candle in the darkness can be a refreshing focal point for churches generally focused on screens. Occasionally singing *a cappella* will be an aural treat for those used to thundering organs or loud drums. Cutting down an over-cluttered order of service and leading times of silence

---

152 John 12:1-8.

or recorded instrumental music can facilitate peace in a busy week.[153]

All of those ideas above are simple and sustainable in most churches. Here is another very simple creative worship experience which we have found powerful in the past.

⏱ PAUSE TO WORSHIP

Collage reflection

Gather together a pile of old magazines or newspapers, a piece of plain paper and some glue (try this on your own now, but you can also do it in a group). Think about where you are at with God at the moment. Look through the magazines and tear out any pictures or words which reflect your current relationship with God. If you are doing this in a group, invite people to share their pictures and pray for one another. If you are on your own, take a moment to talk to God about the collage you have created.

Every time we have used this idea, we have been surprised at how easily people who are self-proclaimed non-creatives engage with it. The collages beautifully reflect people's personalities: some will glue together straight lines of words, whereas others will focus on textures and colours. The 'given' images from the magazines open up different ways of seeing and understanding our lives.

---

153 For more ideas like this, see our book *Simple Worship* (Music and Worship Foundation, 2016).

CHARACTER TYPES AND GIFTS

Beyond the five senses, you can also consider the different kinds of people you have in your congregation. We have already said that Jesus communicated in different ways depending on his audience. To what extent do we know the different kinds of people in our congregations? Does your church make space for introverts and extroverts, quiet people and noisy types, thinkers and feelers, traditionalists and innovators? How could we shape our worship to connect effectively with each one?

One way of looking at this is to think about learning styles or 'modes'. The VARK system suggests that most people are some kind of mix of these different approaches to communication:

- Visual
- Auditory (hearing)
- Reading and writing
- Kinaesthetic (touch and learning by doing)[154]

If you imagine your typical Sunday service, which learning modes do you tend towards? Our experiences tell us that the Auditory style is primary - we speak, pray verbally, sing and preach. You could estimate that this is perhaps 80% of our intentional communication. And yet, surveys show that only 20% of people have Auditory as their primary learning mode.[155] This would suggest that our communication is far

154 http://vark-learn.com
155 See Marlene LeFever, *Learning Styles: Reaching Everyone God Gave You to Teach* (Kingsway, 1995) page 154.

from as effective as it might be! On the positive side, we have found that actively including a range of learning modes is both manageable and also helps break down previous barriers of age and background within the congregation.[156]

What would your worship times look like if you intentionally engaged different learning modes? One implication might be that you would need to draw on a wider range of gifts and art-forms. We have already touched on the fact that there are gifts within your congregation which may not currently be encouraged. Andy Flannagan shared with us:

> The thing that breaks my heart is that we've confined the role of leadership in worship to the person with the guitar or the keyboard, and thereby we're losing a whole generation of potential worship leaders who are incredibly gifted in dance, poetry or other forms of creative expression. And there's this beautiful thing that happens the first time you see someone like that leading others in worship.[157]

---

156 For more resource books on this kind of varied worship see Dan Kimball and Lilly Lewin, *Sacred Space* (Youth Specialties, 2008) and Bob Rognlien, *Experiential Worship* (NavPress, 2005).

157 Andy Flannagan, interview for the *How Would Jesus Lead Worship* video course.

🔆 IDEAS TO TRY

Using other gifts and learning modes

• **Visual**: Do you have people in your church who take photographs, or can create engaging PowerPoint slides? Are there people who can film and edit video, or make animations? All of these can be used in worship, for example as visual prompts to pray for situations,[158] or to communicate a Bible passage,[159] or to tell a testimony in a fresh way. Alternatively, for a low-tech approach you could ask someone to gather visual props to illustrate points or inspire prayer.

• **Auditory**: Beyond the usual preaching/praying/singing, are there other auditory art-forms you could use? Look out for people gifted in poetry, rap, liturgy or other spoken-word performance.[160] There are many examples of creative writing like this on our website.[161] You may have musicians who don't fit so well into a 'worship band' setting, but could play instrumental music for times of reflection, or people skilled at choosing just the right recorded music for a particular moment. One of our friends is a Sound Artist, and plays overlapping recordings of Bible passages read by different voices to highlight the harmony and dissonances of texts.[162]

---

158 See https://engageworship.org/dehumanised
159 See Richard Lyall's Visual Readings here: https://engageworship.org/VisualReadings
160 Gerard Kelly's book *Spoken Worship* (Zondervan, 2007) is great for this. Also check out Dai Woolridge's https://spoken-truth.com
161 See https://engageworship.org/CreativeWriting
162 Read and hear more about Sunil's Bible sound art here - http://www.

• **Reading and writing**: You can create moments for people to pause and engage with a printed sheet. This could be themed around a Bible passage, and involve questions that prompt prayer and reflection. This can be perceived as the kind of thing we only use with children, but adults with a reading/writing learning style can find it a much easier way of processing than being asked to keep everything in their minds.[163]

• **Kinaesthetic**: Teachers are often experts at this, because they are aware that so many children learn better while using their hands (what we might dismiss as 'fiddling'). There are also likely to be just as many adults in your congregation who would appreciate a more active, hands-on approach to worship. We have given out pipe cleaners and asked congregations to shape things relevant to our theme. Sign language and physical posture can also be used very effectively - asking people to use their hands and bodies in prayer and response.[164]

CREATIVE WORSHIP IN A TEAM

If you treat creative worship as a solo sport you will quickly be discouraged and exhausted. However, if you work with other people you will find it a transformative team activity. As a team you can encourage one another, honing and shaping half-formed ideas into glorious life. Look around for people

---

sunilchandy.com. We used one of Sunil's recordings as part of these prayer stations: https://engageworship.org/prayer-hunt

163 See https://engageworship.org/ScribbleSheets

164 See https://engageworship.org/hand-prayers

in your community who can bring a fresh angle, a new skill or just a willing pair of hands to make things happen, and get them together around a cup of tea to dream up creative worship.

It is, of course, possible to pull creative ideas straight from websites or resource books (and we welcome you to use and adapt the ones we share!). But there is something very special about worship generated from within a community. If creative worship is 'indigenous', drawing from the gifts and experiences of that congregation and the location it finds itself in, it will have far more impact than only pulling ideas 'off the shelf'. Eileen Crowley writes:

> After years of thinking about the intersection of worship and media, researching actual community practices, and teaching graduate theology students and pastors about media art in worship, I have come to this conclusion: The more local the creation of the media art, the greater the spiritual fruits for the worshiping community. [...] 'Go local,' I plead with all who will listen. The creation and reception of liturgical media art can become an ever-deepening spiritual practice that can potentially engage the entire community.[165]

She goes on to unpack how collaborating together on a creative worship project is a transformative process for the team involved. It means wrestling over Bible texts and their

165 Eileen D. Crowley, 'Of Devices, Focal Practices, and Mystery', *Liturgy*, 23:3, pages 51-56.

application for today. It means asking searching questions about art-forms, images, sounds and experiences. It means disagreeing, failing, forgiving and growing in relationships. The result is that the creation of worship activities can be as fruitful for discipleship as using them in a service.

THE PARK CHURCH EXPERIENCE

This has been our experience as we have collaborated with friends over a fresh expression of church in a park.[166] We have met twice a month over the last three years, to explore what indigenous worship looks like when you are surrounded by trees, squirrels and see-saws rather than walls, windows and chairs.

Each member of the team has different skills - some know lots about the natural world and can help us see glimpses of God in his creation. Others are good at writing prayers that work outdoors with no screens or books. Some turn games like kite-flying and hide-and-seek into fun spiritual exercises. And some team members can show how the Bible sounds different when you read it (as it was often originally written and read) in an outdoor space.[167] The best sessions are when these different skills work together.

This kind of collaborative, indigenous worship has produced some interesting fruit:

---

166 http://www.parkchurchluton.com
167 If you would like to explore some worship outside, check out our book *Outdoor Worship* (Music and Worship Foundation, 2015).

- All ages worship together on an even footing outdoors. Children are more engaged, less distracted, and there is space for everyone to contribute.
- It is easy and natural to incorporate aspects of everyday life into our worship. Sticks, snails, bubbles, birds and rubbish have all featured in our sessions, and we are more appreciative and caring of the stuff of God's creation as a result.
- Worship changes with the seasons as the year progresses. We engage with God differently in the cold of the snow than we do in the heat of the summer.
- Working together means we get good feedback from each other on what worked, and how things can be improved in the future.

Worshipping in a park might be a long way from your context, but these principles can also be applied to wherever you find yourself. Ask God to show you who you could partner with in developing collaborative, local and creative worship.

COMMUNION: THE SUPREME ACT OF CREATIVE WORSHIP?

If we are honest, we know that there have been moments when we've resented accommodating Communion into Sunday worship. It may cut down the time for sung worship, or perhaps the use of the Communion table involves moving the musical gear and fitting into a smaller space - how inconvenient!

We must somehow break through our overfamiliarity with the Lord's Supper, to be reminded that this is the act of worship *Jesus himself* gave us. Perhaps the traditions we have built around it, although not bad in themselves, have made it stale. For some, the notion of it being a meal of 'remembrance' might have distracted us from Communion as a place where we can encounter God through Jesus by the Spirit, just as much as we might in songs or teaching. As James Torrance writes:

> The trinitarian view sees the Lord's Supper as the supreme expression of all worship. It is the act in which the risen and ascended Lord meets us at his table, in the power of the Spirit, to bring his passion to our remembrance, and to draw us to himself that we may share his communion with the Father and his intercessions for the world.[168]

Not only is this the act of worship given by Jesus, but it also offers us a model of how multi-sensory and creative worship might look. It is striking that Jesus did not give us a song or a creed - he gave us a meal. This was, on one hand, a very ordinary everyday thing, to sit around a table with friends and eat bread and wine. Every day across the world people share meals, and for many, bread continues to be a staple. Each time we eat it, we can remember him.

But as we've seen before, Jesus does not stop with simple, everyday elements. He adds to them a depth and a resonance, drawing from Jewish history and his own future. We should remember that Jesus shared his last supper on Passover night,[169]

---

168 Torrance, *Worship, Community and the Triune God of Grace*, pages 10–11.
169 Luke 22:7–20.

one of the most important festivals in the Jewish calendar. At this feast they remembered their escape from Egypt, when the blood of the sacrificial lamb was placed on the doors of their houses so that the judgement of God would 'pass over' them. Jesus does not explicitly draw the parallel between this lamb and his own death, but it must have been in the minds of those reflecting on events at the time.[170] Even before Jesus' death, the meal was potent with symbolism.

Jesus takes the symbolism further, however. It was traditional for the youngest son (note God's concern for people of all ages to understand) to ask the father of the household questions about the significance of the night and the food they were eating.[171] Jesus uses these 'teaching moments' to load the symbolic elements of bread and wine with even more meaning:

> 'This is my body given for you; do this in remembrance
> of me.' In the same way, after the supper he took the
> cup, saying, 'This cup is the new covenant in my blood,
> which is poured out for you.' *(Luke 22:19–20)*

He takes the familiar elements and applies them to himself; affirming their existing significance but also transforming them in the light of his imminent death and resurrection. He gives us a multi-sensory worship experience which is simple and repeatable, yet so deep and profound that we will never tire of exploring its riches.

---

170 Paul speaks of Jesus as the Passover Lamb in 1 Corinthians 5:7–8.
171 Green, *Luke*, page 758.

☀ IDEAS TO TRY

Everyday objects

Here are some examples of how we can be like Jesus in using objects people interact with each day - mobile phones, chocolate and coffee, plant pots - and turn them into parables, prayers or illustrations of the kingdom. These simple ideas also mean that when your congregation come across these objects in their week they will be reminded of God's presence with them.

Turn off all the lights to make the church as dark as you can. Then ask people to switch on their mobile phones, using just this faint light to reflect on John 1:5: 'The light shines in the darkness, but the darkness has not overcome it.'

Hand out Fairtrade coffee beans and ask people to eat them while reflecting on the bitterness of unfair trade. Then distribute Fairtrade chocolate, and invite people to think about the sweetness of justice as they eat it. Finally pray for God to be at work in these issues.

Provide plant pots, soil, seed and water. Encourage people to meditate on John 12:24, plant the seed and then consider that in their own lives they need the water of the Spirit, the light of God, and the feeding of his word to enable them to grow. They can take the pots home as a reminder in their everyday lives.

WIDENING THE FEAST

We have seen that not only did Jesus use everyday objects in worship, but he also respected and drew from the Jewish spiritual tradition in which he had been raised. In our rush to be relevant to the world around us, as worship leaders we are sometimes in danger of ignoring 2000 years of Christian tradition in favour of the latest fad. It is as if we have just discovered pizza, and in our enthusiasm have started serving it at every meal. In a similar way, we run the risk of serving our congregations with only one form of worship. We must not forget all the other songs, prayers and acts from across church history and the world today which would broaden our worship diet.

There is a vast richness in exploring historic worship like Celtic liturgy[172] or prayers from the early Church, which might focus people on God in a fresh way. There are powerful reflective practices from the Contemplative tradition you could incorporate into your service,[173] and many other strands of worship from around the world. We need to do our best to understand these in their own context, and work out appropriate ways they might enhance our usual service patterns.

As well as prayers and practices, the church has also produced an enormous range of music in the past 2000 years. It is very easy to get stuck in a rut of using songs from a narrow range of writers and eras. Exploring the wealth of hymns from

172 For Celtic worship resources, visit www.northumbriacommunity.org and www.faithandworship.com

173 See ideas in our book *Simple Worship*, pages 49-65.

the past is an almost unending source of potential material. You may find it helpful to carefully revise lyrics to make them understandable,[174] add a chorus or refrain, and 'retune'[175] or at least reharmonise music to fit your context. We often do this, and are so grateful for the way hymns like 'To God Be The Glory', 'Breathe on Me Breath of God' and 'Immortal, Invisible' lead our worship in fresh directions.

Beyond hymns, there is also a breadth of music styles from around the world which we can benefit from. Many churches in non-Western contexts are united in singing songs from the UK, USA and Australia, but we feel that the flow ought to also go the other way. Personally, we have learned new perspectives from worshipping with brothers and sisters in Peru, and when we use Peruvian songs in the UK church they contribute something unique. Living in Luton also means we have gained so much from our British-African friends who have taught us new rhythms, tunes and ways of engaging with God with our whole selves. Singing the simple, repeated chants of the ecumenical Taizé community in France[176] adds another distinctive and much-needed flavour to our worship feast.

As always, the best place to start with this kind of thing is to look around you. Do you have someone in your church from another culture? Ask them to teach you a song, or share a YouTube clip. Is there a person who comes from a different church tradition, or is knowledgeable about a particular strand of Christian spirituality? Invite them to share an aspect of that

---

174 See jubilate.co.uk for examples of updated texts.
175 https://cardiphonia.org/2012/01/31/the-top-30-retuned-hymns/
176 http://www.taize.fr/

in worship. Don't look to radically change your church's style overnight, but instead take small steps towards a wider and more nourishing diet.

MAKING A START

Introducing creative worship in your church should be more about evolution than revolution. We have found it best to 'drip feed' new ideas into our existing service patterns, looking for the easiest connection points and working from there. Everyone has been made by God to respond creatively, but this does not have to look any one particular way. Every church and every person will have some worship expressions they find more natural, and others which are more of a challenge. Identify what is 'indigenous', a heart response for at least some people in your community, and be creative there. As you gradually introduce more creative elements into your services, people will become more and more comfortable with the idea of worshipping in multi-sensory and varied ways.

As you are doing this, be aware of making your creative worship accessible for everyone. Be mindful of the abilities and struggles of people in your community as you plan things, and avoid excluding those with particular needs. For example, if you are asking people to pick up stones and put them in a bucket, are there enough stones? Would putting them on a table be more accessible for those with limited mobility than leaving them on the floor? Similarly, if you have people with limited eyesight or reading level, consider how they might engage with a response which involves reading from a screen.

You could read this aloud first, or give out large print handouts, or include another sense apart from just seeing.

When you are leading congregations into creative elements, make sure to invite and encourage, don't order and demand. Make space for people to opt-out of what you are suggesting. We often say 'You might find it helpful to...' or 'We'd like to invite you to...' We try to give more than one option if the activity might be difficult for some people, for example if a response involves moving around the building we might include a second alternative of staying in your seat and reflecting on a PowerPoint presentation. If you are concerned that people may be nervous to be the first to respond to an activity, it can help to prime a few confident people to go first. Try things out, be gracious with yourself when things don't go quite the way you planned, and learn from your experiences.

⏱ PAUSE TO WORSHIP

Tiny seeds

We began this chapter by reflecting on Jesus' use of the tiny mustard seed. If you can, find a mustard seed or another small seed and hold it in your hand.

When you think about creative worship, it may feel like what you have to bring is a tiny seed. You may consider your artistic, or musical, or leadership gifts to be small and insignificant. People might have discouraged you in your gifts, or you might have tried creative projects which didn't go the way you planned. As you hold the seed in your hand, talk to God about how you feel.

Once you have been honest with God, you may wish to pause and listen for his response to you.

To close your time, speak this prayer to God:

God, I hold this seed in my hand.
I see smallness, weakness, insignificance.
You see potential, growth, significance.

Tiny seeds grow by your power into huge trees.
They provide food for the hungry and homes for the birds.
From the darkness of the earth springs forth your life, your harvest.

Your kingdom is like a tiny seed.

When I look at your church, my own life, my gifts,
I see smallness, weakness, insignificance.
You see potential, growth, significance.
Give me eyes of faith and willing hands to see your
kingdom grow in me.

May I plant the seeds of my creativity with faith,
nurture them in community,
and see you use them for your glory,
gathering the harvest your love has provided.

In Christ's name and the power of the Spirit
I commit myself to you again.
Amen.[177]

---

177 This prayer is adapted from a corporate one, available here - https://
engageworship.org/tiny-seeds

CHAPTER 6

RELIANT ON THE SPIRIT

If we were to invite you to a time of Spirit-filled worship, what kind of meeting would you expect it to be? Like a lot of language in the Church, mentioning the Holy Spirit seems to have become a shorthand for a particular style, so you would probably anticipate an unstructured service with long times of modern music.

Let us tell you a story that turns that expectation on its head a little bit. One year, Sara was leading a small prayer gathering at a Christian conference. This conference had plenty of loud sung-worship times and enthusiastic prayer ministry going on around the site, so we wanted to provide something different. Sara introduced the meeting by explaining that she would facilitate two quiet, contemplative exercises. At that point - we found out later - an older lady in the back row turned to her friend and whispered that this kind of stuff was not for her and she wanted to leave. The friend wanted to stay, however, so the lady stuck around, somewhat reluctantly.

Sara guided the group in a simple Bible meditation, reading through a passage of Scripture slowly and asking God to reveal himself through his word. On the back row, our reluctant guest began to experience some strange symptoms: she felt warm waves travelling through her, waves of love and peace. She turned to her friend again and whispered: 'I don't know what's going on, I'm feeling this heat welling up within me!' Her friend, who had experienced something similar in the past, replied that she believed the lady was being filled with the Holy Spirit. And so they prayed together at the back.

Sara knew nothing about any of this until the back row ladies came forward at the end and explained what had happened. Sara had not planned or advertised this session as 'Being filled with the Spirit', there was little to no singing, certainly no band and even the Bible passage she used was about something else. But God had other plans. The Holy Spirit is not constrained by our (often too small) expectations!

The Spirit is not a kind of accessory for a certain type of Christian, like a rainbow guitar strap, a fish car sticker, or a 'What Would Jesus Do?' bracelet. He is, rather, at the core of our faith and at the heart of all Christian worship. And in this chapter we will explore how Jesus' life in Luke can inspire us for truly Spirit-filled worship - worship which sends us out empowered to live for God. As Tom Wright expresses it:

> Luke's overall narrative informs us that the Spirit
> inspires the worship of the church, the worship that
> stakes the astonishing claim to be the reality to which

the Temple-worship was pointing all along, and thereby enables the church to be the missionary community.[178]

JESUS AND THE SPIRIT

We saw in Chapter 2 that although Jesus was fully God, he was also fully human and so had to be fully reliant on the Holy Spirit to live a life of perfect worship. We might think of the Trinity as an abstract theological concept for the academics to concern themselves with, but really, every act Jesus did was a trinitarian act - Jesus the Son, doing the will of the Father, by the Holy Spirit. As Peter explains in the book of Acts,

> 'God anointed Jesus of Nazareth with the Holy Spirit and power, and [...] he went around doing good and healing all who were under the power of the devil, because God was with him.' *(Acts 10:38)*

Luke mentions the Holy Spirit more than any other Gospel writer and shows how Jesus was fully reliant on the Spirit throughout his life: Jesus did not bring himself to the earth but was conceived by the Spirit,[179] the Spirit anointed him at his baptism,[180] he was led and empowered by the Holy Spirit

---

178 NT Wright, 'Worship and the Spirit in the New Testament' in Teresa Berger, Bryan D Spinks (eds) *The Spirit in Worship - Worship in the Spirit* (Liturgical Press, 2009) pages 3-24. Wright argues that 'When we look at the Spirit and worship in the new Testament we find that the early Christians believed that their Spirit-led worship was the new-covenantal form of that synagogue and Temple worship, worshipping the same creator God but filling that worship with new content relating specifically to Jesus crucified and risen - and believing [...] that the promised Holy Spirit was leading them in that worship.' Page 6.

179 Luke 1:35.

180 Luke 3:22.

during his temptations in the desert,[181] and he proclaimed that the Spirit was at the very core of his identity and mission, anointing him to preach and heal.[182]

In addition, the book of Hebrews shows us that on the cross Jesus offered himself by the Spirit, presenting a perfect sacrifice:

> How much more, then, will the blood of Christ, who
> *through the eternal Spirit* offered himself unblemished
> to God, cleanse our consciences from acts that
> lead to death, so that we may serve the living God!
> *(Hebrews 9:14, emphasis added)*

Paul tells us that even in Jesus' resurrection he was raised by the Father through the Spirit.[183] And remarkably, in the same breath, Pauls tells the Romans that *we* are included as beneficiaries in this powerful act of God:

> And if the Spirit of him who raised Jesus from the dead
> is living in you, he who raised Christ from the dead will
> also give life to your mortal bodies because of his Spirit
> who lives in you. *(Romans 8:11)*

The same Spirit who empowered Jesus' perfect life of worship and raised Christ from the dead can be found *in us!*[184] We can be filled with that same presence of God to join in Jesus'

---

181 Luke 4:1, 14.

182 Luke 4:18–19.

183 Romans 1:4; 8:11.

184 See also Ephesians 1:18–20.

worship of the Father. All Christians have the Spirit of Christ inside them, every act of Christian worship is 'in the Spirit',[185] and the deeper we delve into this, the more we will be released to worship as Jesus leads us.

We need to stop thinking of the Holy Spirit as being on the periphery of church worship, concerned only with charismatic phenomena and manifestations. Just as he empowered Jesus for a life of perfect worship, so he wants to empower us too, to be like Jesus in our lives and acts of worship.

THE SPIRIT AS THE 'DYNAMIS' OF GOD

> One day Jesus was teaching, and Pharisees and teachers of the law were sitting there. They had come from every village of Galilee and from Judea and Jerusalem. And *the power of the Lord was with Jesus* to heal those who were ill. *(Luke 5:17, emphasis added)*

This is the introduction to the story about Jesus healing the paralysed man who was lowered through the roof. It sets the story up by explaining that the power of God was present in Jesus to do acts of healing. The word for 'power' here is the Greek word *dynamis*, from which we get words like 'dynamic' and 'dynamite'. It's the same word used in Luke 24:19, when the disciples on the road to Emmaus describe Jesus as 'a prophet, powerful in word and deed', and then in verse 49, where the disciples are commanded by Jesus, 'Stay in the city until you have been clothed with power from on high.' With

185 Philippians 3:3.

Acts 2 at the back of our minds, we know that this 'power
from on high' was to be the Holy Spirit.

From Luke 5:17 it should be clear, then, that Jesus did not
muster up in himself power to heal; it was not a case of blind
faith or trying a little harder. It is the Holy Spirit who makes
possible the presence of God's power on earth. Luke Timothy
Johnson translates the last sentence in this verse as 'The power
of the Lord was enabling him to heal.'[186] Jesus was, as we have
stressed before, fully God, but he limited himself to live as a
fully human being, and for that reason he relied on the Holy
Spirit to do his acts of kingdom power.

If that was true for Jesus, how much more do we need to
rely fully on the Spirit, to live for God, to worship God and to
lead others in worship? And yet, in church, we can act as if it's
more about ambience, songs or diligent planning.

In Acts, Luke gives us a fuller report of Jesus' final words
to the disciples:

> 'Do not leave Jerusalem, but wait for the gift my Father
> promised, which you have heard me speak about. For
> John baptised with water, but in a few days you will be
> baptised with the Holy Spirit.' *(Acts 1:4–5)*

Probably the hardest word for many of us to hear in that
passage is 'wait'. We can be so eager to rush into times of
worship leading; relying on rehearsal, musical skill, the PA
system and the words on the screen. How often do we take
time to wait on God, to rely on his Spirit? How often do we

---

186 Luke Timothy Johnson, *The Gospel of Luke* (Liturgical Press, 1991) page 91.

wait to hear God's still, small voice before we launch into the next spectacular time of ministry? American worship leader Manuel Luz, in his challenging book *Honest Worship,* writes:

> Here is my fear for the church: in the midst of all the smoke machines, the high-def video loops, and the latest worship hits, we may be settling for something less than true transcendence, something less than Spirit-breathed worship, something less than God on God's terms.[187]

LEARNING TO RELY ON THE SPIRIT

A few years ago, we went away on a church weekend. It was a busy time, as we loaded piles of equipment into a van and spent hours rigging, sound checking and rehearsing around the packed schedule of meetings and meals. Everything looked and sounded great, but somewhere towards the end of the weekend, Sam began to feel uneasy. He realised he was choosing songs less for their relevance or because of God's leading, and more because he felt they would 'work' - inspiring hand-raising, loud singing or some other reaction from the congregation. He realised that not once over the whole weekend had we prayed together as a music group. It felt as if the worship had been empty and shallow.

These concerns about our church worship were confirmed when, a week later, two ladies grabbed Sara after she had just led a time of singing. 'Sara!' they enthused, 'Your

187 Manuel Luz, *Honest Worship: From False Self to True Praise* (IVP, 2018) page 14.

singing was so wonderful today! We didn't feel like we needed to sing ourselves at all. We were just caught up in the sound of your voice!' The alarm bells rang louder in our heads. Were we relying on our technology and skills so much, and the Holy Spirit so little, that our worship had become a shallow performance?

We knew that drastic measures were called for, so, for the next few months (which coincidentally ran into Lent), we stripped back all our singing in services to simple songs accompanied by just a guitar or piano, or no instruments at all. Meanwhile, we turned our weekly band practice over to a 90-minute prayer time, to seek God, ask his forgiveness and pray for the worship life of the church. We invited the Holy Spirit to fill us once again, that we might be led by him to worship the Father through what Jesus has done. We intentionally put our reliance back on him to bring depth and life to our worship.[188]

When we eventually reinstated our bands for Easter, the fruit of praying together was clearly apparent, as was the effect on our congregations of getting used to worshipping without a band. Worship felt like more of a corporate act again than an individual performance. We weren't trying to manipulate anyone or second-guess God's will, but we let his Spirit take control. It is a lesson that we have to keep coming back to; to humble ourselves before God, telling him that we are totally reliant on his Holy Spirit to bring life and meaning to our worship.

---

188 For more on stripping back your worship to better rely on God, see our resource book *Simple Worship*.

🕐 PAUSE TO WORSHIP

Come Holy Spirit

Find a piece of paper and write down all the things you think you may rely on in place of the Holy Spirit, both in your everyday life and in your worship leading. What earthly things do you find security in - money, technology, natural talents, your job title or position...? Ask God for forgiveness where you have not trusted in him first.

Then spend some time reflecting on these four verses of the *Veni, Creator Spiritus*, an ancient prayer attributed to the monk and theologian Rabanus Maurus (776– 856). You could sing it, write it out in your own hand with decorations, or engage in some other creative or meditative process. You can also find recordings online of this being sung to Gregorian Chant. Ask the Holy Spirit to fill you and empower you to trust him.

Come, Holy Spirit, Creator blest,
and in our souls take up Thy rest;
come with Thy grace and heavenly aid
to fill the hearts which Thou hast made.

O comforter, to Thee we cry,
O heavenly gift of God Most High,
O fount of life and fire of love,
and sweet anointing from above.

Kindle our sense from above,
and make our hearts o'erflow with love;

with patience firm and virtue high
the weakness of our flesh supply.

Now to the Father and the Son,
who rose from death, be glory given,
with Thou, O Holy Comforter,
henceforth by all in earth and heaven. Amen.[189]

WORSHIPPING BY THE SPIRIT

> At that time Jesus, full of joy through the Holy Spirit,
> said, 'I praise you, Father, Lord of heaven and earth'.
> *(Luke 10:21)*

Tom Wright translates these words, 'There and then Jesus
celebrated in the Holy Spirit',[190] while another commentator
explains that '"in the Holy Spirit" here means "under the
influence of" the Holy Spirit'.[191] We find it remarkable that
even *Jesus himself* was inspired by the Spirit to worship. He
was filled with joy by the Spirit to celebrate God's goodness.

This Spirit-filling for special times of worship is not
limited to Jesus. Luke uses very similar words to speak of both
Elizabeth and Mary as they launch into prayers (or songs) of

---

189 Translated text from Francis X. Weiser, S.J, *Handbook of Christian Feasts
and Customs* (Harcourt, Brace and Company, 1958). For more on this prayer see
Theresa Berger's chapter 'Veni Creator Spiritus' in *The Spirit in Worship*, page 141.
190 Wright, *Luke for Everyone*, page 123.
191 Johnson, *The Gospel of Luke*, page 169.

praise.[192] Zechariah is also filled with the Spirit to sing his prophetic worship song.[193]

Of course, all Christian worship must be empowered by the Spirit, whether it is planned or spontaneous, traditional or contemporary. But it remains true that at certain times the Holy Spirit makes himself known in more obvious ways. Perhaps the best-known biblical example is in Acts 4:31, where the disciples are worshipping and the whole place is shaken by the Spirit.

As we think about all these examples, a pattern emerges. In Luke 10, Jesus' Spirit-filled worship is a response to the disciples' successful mission trip and his vision of Satan falling from heaven. Elizabeth and Mary are responding to the news of Jesus' conception and God's choice of the least over the greatest. Zechariah praises God for fulfilling his promise of a redeemer for Israel and for the birth of his own son, John, who will play a part in this redemption. We begin to see here that the Holy Spirit often inspires 'revelation' which leads to a 'response': people's praise is rooted in a fresh understanding or realisation of the truth of God.[194]

As leaders of worship, we need to think through the implications of this pattern. We might assume that creating a mood with a certain style of music or selection of songs will inspire worship in the Spirit, but (without downplaying the power or significance of appropriate music) the fact remains

---

192 Luke 1:41, 46–55.

193 Luke 1:67–79.

194 Ralph P. Martin, *The Worship Of God: Some Theological, Pastoral and Practical Reflections* (Eerdmans, 1994) page 10.

that there must be more to our worship than this. If Spirit-filled worship is a response to revelation, we need to make space for the truth of God to be freshly revealed to people, and think about how we can facilitate this revelation.

☀ IDEAS TO TRY

Revelation to spark response

• **Song Lyrics:** Some worship songs are all response: 'I will'; 'I feel'; 'We bow...'. This is important, but the exhale of breathing also requires an inhale. When you are choosing songs, find some which contain revelation - the story of God's activity in the world, the good news of the gospel. This might be found in classic hymns, or in songs which remind the congregation of who God is and what he has done. It will then be natural to go from the inhale of information into the exhale of response.

• **Testimony:** If you know people in your congregation with stories of God's faithfulness, why not invite them to share during a time of worship? One way we have done this is to ask everyone in the congregation to write on a slip of paper one thing for which they want to give thanks to God. Then we have used a simple song like the chorus of Rich Mullins' 'Awesome God' or Chris Tomlin's 'How Great is our God' and interspersed each chorus with readings from the slips of paper. This inspires worship as a genuine response to what God is doing among you.[195]

---

195 https://www.engageworship.org/testimonies-praise

- **Bible Readings:** A carefully chosen passage, perhaps read over the top of instrumental music or projected on a screen with inspiring images as a background, can remind the congregation of God's truths. Allow space for the Holy Spirit to bring the passage to life and inspire people to worship in response to it.

- **Response to Sermons:** How much thought do you give to songs or other forms of worship in response to the talk? Do you leave space for the Holy Spirit to apply the word to people's lives, perhaps with silence, instrumental music or a guided meditation? How can worship flow as an active response to God's word?

ASKING FOR THE SPIRIT

When our daughter Ella was just a baby, she was given a small, fuzzy, mechanical cow as a Christmas gift. If you turned on the switch on the cow's stomach, the toy made a twitchy attempt at walking and let out a sound which was supposed to be a 'moo' but actually sounded more like a circular saw slicing wood. Unsurprisingly, Ella was petrified by it. Around the same time, Ella had perfected the art of crawling and had begun taking full advantage of her new mobility by speedily making her way over to the rubbish bin and tipping out its content. Something had to be done, and we decided to use Ella's fear to our advantage - our only defence for this is our sleep-deprived state - by placing the scary cow as a guard in front of the bin. For a little while our floor was kept clean, but soon, as first time parents, we worried that we were causing our daughter long-term trauma. So after a day or so, we instigated a reconciliation session where Ella got to touch the cow and discover that it wasn't dangerous, and that she didn't need to fear. Back to the dirty floor again!

A good gift, misunderstood, became an object of fear and a barrier for Ella. For too many Christians, the Holy Spirit is a bit like that. Some people are afraid or worried about him; perhaps they think he will cause uncontrolled or weird manifestations, or they might have been part of a church where so-called 'spiritual' occurrences were manipulated or insensitively handled. Other people might want to experience more of the Holy Spirit but feel that they are not in the élite spiritual 'club', one of those super-Christians who appear to have the Spirit on tap. For anyone who has ever felt any of those fears, these words from Jesus offer consolation.

> 'Which of you fathers, if your son asks for a fish, will give him a snake instead? Or if he asks for an egg, will give him a scorpion? If you then, though you are evil, know how to give good gifts to your children, how much more will your Father in heaven give the Holy Spirit to those who ask him!' *(Luke 11:11–13)*

The message is that our Father longs to give us his Holy Spirit, because he loves us and wants the best for us. Of course, if we are Christians, the Holy Spirit is already inside us, but if we are feeling dry and thirsty for more of him, Jesus promises that the Spirit will well up within us.[196] The Holy Spirit is not for the

---

196 John 7:37–39.

'spiritually élite' (and anyone who sets themselves up as such is probably best avoided); he is for everyone, regardless of whether they have mystical experiences or supernatural feelings. The real test of being Spirit-filled is if we are empowered to live and worship more like Jesus.[197]

We see from Luke 11:5–10, immediately preceding the passage quoted above, that we need to keep asking, seeking and knocking at God's door for the Holy Spirit, like a friend persistently knocking on another friend's door in the middle of the night. We need to be filled and go on being filled.[198] This is true for us as individuals and also corporately as we seek God to pour out more of his Spirit into our church worship. We should 'always pray and not give up' (18:1) for God to reveal more of himself.

If you, for whatever reason, feel afraid of the Holy Spirit, read again Jesus' reassuring words above. He frames asking for the Spirit in the most ordinary, everyday universal language there is - a kid asking their parent for a snack. And the Father, of course, willingly responds. Unlike us, he is the perfect parent and he won't give us something scary or unhelpful. The Holy Spirit is a good gift, not sent to frighten or harm us. In our experience we have found the Holy Spirit to be very kind and compassionate, even considerate - he will only come into the parts of our lives where we invite him in. Our God is a God of order, not chaos.[199] As leaders in the church, we should be careful to make space for the Holy Spirit, but also to be

197 Galatians 5:22– 25.
198 Ephesians 5:18.
199 1 Corinthians 14:31–33.

pastorally wise and sensitive about how services are run, so that everyone is brought along together and God's peace rules.

THE SPIRIT AND SPONTANEITY

Order, peace and pastoral sensitivity are all important. But these things should not be shackles attempting to control the Holy Spirit. The Apostle Paul says:

> Now the Lord is the Spirit, and where the Spirit of the Lord is, there is freedom. *(2 Corinthians 3:17)*

Jesus compares those 'born of the Spirit' to the untameable wind, blowing wherever it pleases.[200] As you read through the gospels, it is striking how Jesus is always able to respond with just the right words or actions in the moment. He is not bound by tradition or expectation - he is free and spontaneous as he is led by God's Spirit.

Spontaneity is another aspect of Spirit-filled worship which many churches would like to grow in. We often get into conversations with worship leaders who would like to see their gatherings released to respond to what God is doing in that moment. They confess not knowing how to practically create this kind of space. In our experience, spontaneity in worship is the coming together of two things:

1. Hearing God speak into the moment by the Holy Spirit
2. Our ability to respond, communicate and act on that word.

---

200 John 3:8.

We need to be working on both of these aspects if we want our services to respond to what God is doing in the moment.

SPONTANEITY PART 1: HEARING GOD SPEAK

The first part of growing in spontaneity is the ability to sense God's guiding during the service. Of course, we ought to take time to listen for God's guidance in our planning and preparation as much as in the service. But being attentive to God during the actual leading of worship allows God to guide and shape the meeting as it unfolds.

This is a helpful mindset to have, because it reminds us who is really in control of the service. It stops us being too reliant on our own planning and skills. Being open to God during the meeting should also make you attentive to what is going on around you - this is why we will often keep our eyes open when leading worship. God can reveal things as you look around the room. As well as physical sight you can also start to 'see' with the eyes of your heart that he is taking the worship time in a certain direction.

Many people are unsure of quite how to discern God's guidance. For us, we have found that to grow in our ability to hear God's direction we have had to learn to listen to God in our everyday lives. Henri Nouwen writes:

> Prayer is first and foremost listening to Jesus, who dwells in the very depths of your heart. He doesn't shout. He doesn't thrust himself upon you [...]

Whatever you do with your life, go on listening to the voice of Jesus in your heart.[201]

You can listen to God in your morning prayer time, or when faced with a difficult decision at work, or when making family or financial plans, or when you are on a bus. We have found that asking God specific questions rather than just saying 'speak to me Lord' helps us be more attentive to his responses. You can and should do this when you are on your own, but we have found it also helps to do some of this listening with a friend or in a small group. There you can discern together what is God's direction and what is just your own thoughts and feelings.

When you ask God a question, sit quietly and be open to what he might say. In our experience this is never a 'booming' voice, and rarely even distinct words. But it might take the shape of a picture, or a sense, or a Bible passage which pops into our heads. You can test these things by sharing them with your prayer partners, and by God's word in the Bible. You can then begin to act on the things you sense are correct. Things which are from God will make themselves evident in this way, and you will start to become more confident in your listening.

In the context of an actual church service, we can be hindered by assumptions of what 'spontaneity' might look like. Just because you've seen freedom in the Spirit be manifest one way in another church, doesn't mean that is what God will do in your congregation. Be open to all kinds of different ways

201 Henri Nouwen, *Letters to Marc* (DLT, 1988) pages 76-77.

he might speak. For example, some ways that God could work spontaneously through you might include:

- Giving an instruction to the congregation that you hadn't planned, because it feels right in the moment.
- Singing a song you hadn't planned - either led by you or the congregation.
- Improvised songs or singing in the Spirit.
- Unplanned instrumental sections of music, or other expressions of art and creativity.
- Creating space for spontaneous prayer, possibly in tongues, or other forms of prayer or intercession.
- Having prophetic words spoken - by the leadership or congregation.
- Leaving silence or space for people to receive from God
- ... or something else entirely!

SPONTANEITY PART 2: OUR ABILITY TO RESPOND

Once you have a sense of God's guidance during a worship time, you then need to respond. It is at this point that many of us stumble, unsure of how we can guide our congregations into spontaneous responses. Part of the problem might be over-stuffed services, where we have left no space for God to act outside of our plans. To counter this, consider planning with fewer elements: fewer songs, fewer liturgical aspects, less time given to speakers and so on. Intentionally leave some space to pause, listen, and go where God is leading.

Another element which can inhibit our ability to respond is our confidence and clarity in leading the congregation. For example - you might sense a nudge from God that he wants to come with healing in that moment. How will you guide the congregation into that? What will be appropriate for the context? It could be a case of inviting people to go to a particular corner of the room to be prayed for, or speaking a prayer over the whole congregation, or leading into a song which opens people up to God's work. Do you feel confident to lead into one or more of these activities? We all need to grow in how we invite our churches to respond to God in these situations. Sometimes we will need to make mistakes to learn better practice - make sure you find other leaders who can give you helpful feedback on how you responded to spontaneous moments.

A third area which can hinder our response to spontaneous moments is our musical skills. This applies to both individuals, and to how we work as bands and music groups. Often, the way that we lead is not just about what we say, but how we shape the music in the moment. It may be that you sense God wants to highlight joy and celebration, or a sense of peace and calm, or a discordant feeling of lament. Do you have the musical vocabulary to be able to express these feelings in the way you play? Will you be able to cooperate as a group to transition into that musical mood?

We encourage bands to 'practice spontaneity'. By this we don't mean fake it. We are just aware that it is highly unlikely that you will be able to 'go with the flow' in a service if you've not already experienced doing that in your rehearsals. For example, if every song in rehearsal ends with a pre-defined conclusion, you can't expect your band to tease out the end of a song in the service. So we often practice two or three different endings to a song. We might rehearse a definite stop; a quiet ending which dwells on a couple of chords; a segue into the next song; and so on. We will explain to the band that they need to be aware during the service of how we are leading the ending 'in the moment'. This can help the musicians be prepared for the spontaneous.

Another idea is to intentionally plan too many songs, with the full and clear intention not to play them all. So you might be planning an opening worship time which will begin with a loud song, followed by a mid-tempo song. But then you could have three or four alternatives for your final song, and rehearse them all. Your songwords can be ready on the computer, and everyone is now prepared for what might happen. In the moment you have the freedom to choose between those three or four options, depending on what feels right.

Growing in this area will also involve you learning to communicate well as a music team. Develop simple signals to indicate things like dynamics, repeating a section, jumping to another part of the song and ending the song. Make sure you can all see each other, and learn to look at each other regularly rather than stare at your hands or the chord charts. This can take time, but over the course of a few months you can begin to grow in your ability to play spontaneously together. Improving in these practical areas can have a big spiritual impact.

THE SECRET PLACE OF PRAYER

> The news about him spread all the more, so that crowds of people came to hear him and to be healed of their sicknesses. But Jesus often withdrew to lonely places and prayed. *(Luke 5:15–16)*

When you read through Luke's Gospel, it is remarkable how many times you see Jesus retreating for times of prayer with his Father. When pressure is mounting, it seems that Jesus' need for solitude becomes all the more important. This passage shows that the more success he has in ministry, the more he pulls back to reconnect with his Father. Luke 9:10 tells how Jesus modelled this to his disciples by withdrawing with them after an intense time of ministry. Perhaps the key to Jesus' perfect reliance on the Spirit can be found in these times spent in the secret place of prayer.

In Luke 4:38–44 we read the description of a fairly stressful sabbath in Jesus' life. It starts with teaching and driving out a demon in the synagogue, continues with the healing of Peter's mother-in-law, and, as the day draws to a close, the entire town bring their sick people to Jesus for healing. Where a good night's sleep would be in order for most of us at this point, Jesus leaves to go to a solitary place.[202] What is said between Jesus and the Father at this point? We

---

202 In the parallel passage in Mark 1:35, we learn that his purpose is prayer.

don't know, but somehow he must have had a renewed sense of his identity and calling because, in the following verses, we witness the clarity with which he makes a decision to move on, despite people begging him to stay, 'because that is why I was sent' (Luke 4:43).

Something we have learned while being employed by churches, and later in para-church ministry, is that we cannot rely on church services as our main 'time with God'. Members of the congregation may find Sunday a time of sabbath rest, when they get spiritual input and space to reflect. If you are heavily involved in your church as a volunteer or staff member, you have probably noticed that this doesn't quite work for you. Of course, in serving our congregations we are offering pleasing worship to God, and there may be moments when we can personally connect with him. But in general, when you are thinking about the PA system or musical arrangements, or discerning the pastoral needs of the congregation or a difficult team member, you may not be in the best place to rest in God's presence.

It seems that Jesus had similar experiences in his own ministry. As a result, he set up a pattern of withdrawing to spend time alone with the Father, to be refreshed by him through the Holy Spirit. If we think we can 'fit God in' while prioritising everything else, it is likely that quality time to talk and listen to him will be squeezed out. When we treat our friends or spouses like this they get fed up fairly quickly! Quality relationships need quality time devoted to them, and the only way to do that is to put time with that person in your diary as a priority.

RE-IMAGINING QUIET TIMES

Spending quality time with God in the secret place does not need to be dull or repetitive. You may have grown up with a restrictive idea of what a 'quiet time' must look like - a pattern of Bible reading and prayer that perhaps worked really well for someone else but is ill-fitting for you. In her book *The Gift of Wonder* Christine Aroney-Sine asked the people around her:

> 'What makes you feel close to God?' They responded with stories of sitting by the sea, playing with kids, turning the compost pile, washing the dishes, and walking in the local park. Even taking a shower got a mention. [...] However, they rarely identify these as spiritual practices.[203]

The good news is that God wants you to spend time with him in ways which restore *your* soul and refill *your* creative and spiritual tank. In *Sacred Pathways,* Gary Thomas identifies nine different spiritual 'types' of people, each meeting God in diverse settings.[204] Explore what works for you, whether that be contemplative prayer, creative expressions, deep theological reading, journalling, walks in the woods, singing secret songs with your instrument or something entirely different. It is quite

---

203 Christine Aroney-Sine, *The Gift of Wonder: Creative Practices for Delighting in God* (InterVarsity Press, 2019) page 5.
204 Gary Thomas, *Sacred Pathways: Discover Your Soul's Path to God,* (Zondervan, 2000).

likely that you will click with some mix of these approaches, and that changing your practices with life's seasons will keep things fresh.

Whatever mode you use as you come to God, remember that there is also a wide variety of prayers and postures we can adopt. Some prayer times will be filled with praise and thanks - glorifying God and being grateful for the wonders of his provision. At other times we will need to bring to God our frustrations, disappointments and failures - to lament or ask for forgiveness. We can come in a receiving mode, reading and be refreshed by the Bible or devotional books, or by listening to sermon recordings or inspiring music. We can rest in the presence of the Holy Spirit, receiving his love and knowing the acceptance of our perfect parent. Most of our times alone with God will probably be some kind of mix of talking to him, receiving from him, and the important third aspect of just *being* with him.

IDENTITY FROM THE INSIDE OUT

The most important thing we can do in the secret place is reconnect with our true identity. Who we are, fundamentally, is not reliant on our ministry, gifts or accomplishments. You are not first and foremost a worship leader, or musician, or pastor, or whatever else you do. You are a child of God.

Once, when we were leading a retreat weekend for teenagers and their parents, we showed a clip from one of our favourite films, *Inside Out*. If you've seen the movie you will know it revolves around a cartoon version of how the brain works. The main character is called Riley, and in the clip they demonstrate how important memories build her sense of identity, what they call her 'Islands of Personality'. Riley's identity is made up of a mixture of her favourite pastime (Hockey Island), her relationships (Friendship and Family Islands) and her temperament (Goofball and Honesty Islands).

We encouraged all the guests on the retreat to write or draw their own Islands of Personality on pieces of paper. We talked about how all of these aspects of our lives are important. God is interested in our passions, our hobbies, our successes and our relationships. But, crucially, they are not the totality of who we are. They are not the foundation of who we are. When we define our identity by these things we are on shaky foundations. None of these things are guaranteed to stay the same. They can all be changed, or taken away from us.

In *Inside Out,* Riley moves from Minnesota to San Francisco. Everything that she relied on before as the centre of her identity starts to crumble. All of her islands of personality stop working: she can no longer play on her hockey team; her relationship with her parents breaks down. The things which Riley had based her identity on were good, but they were not enough to sustain her when life got difficult.

There is a firmer foundation than all those other things. Paul writes: 'It's in Christ that we find out who we are and what we are living for' (Ephesians 1:11 MSG).

God doesn't define you by your good works, how much you pray, how much money you give to charity. He doesn't see you first as a musician, or a worship leader, or a pastor, or a creative. He isn't interested mainly in your job title or your success in ministry. He loves you with an unconditional love. An unmerited, unearned favour. He delights in you. This is the firmest foundation to base your identity on.

> Living then, as every one of you does, in pure grace, it's important that you not misinterpret yourselves as people who are bringing this goodness to God. No, God brings it all to you. The only accurate way to understand ourselves is by what God is and by what he does for us, not by what we are and what we do for him. *(Romans 12:3 MSG)*

● PAUSE TO WORSHIP

Islands of personality

Spend some time reflecting on your own Islands of Personality. Write or draw the things that are important to you - hobbies, roles, relationships, accomplishments. How much of your worth and value are wrapped up in these things? To what extent have you tried to make them the foundation of your life?

Spend some time talking to God about this. You may want to ask for forgiveness for where these things have become more important than God in your life.

Having received God's forgiveness, take some time to receive his love and acceptance afresh. You may want to do this using the *Knowing God's Love* episode of our PAUSE/PRAY podcast.[205] Alternatively, find a quiet place and reflect on the following verses. Take the time to dwell on them - turn them over in your mind or write them out for yourself, and allow the truth of them to travel from your head to your heart.

Ephesians 1:11 says that 'God decided ahead of time to choose us through Christ according to his plan.'

Psalm 139:16 says God's eyes saw your unformed body; all the days ordained for you were written in God's book before one of them came to be.

In John 15:9 Jesus says 'As the Father has loved me, so have I loved you. Now remain in my love.'

Colossians 3:12 says you are one of God's chosen people, that you are holy and dearly loved.

In John 15:16 Jesus says 'You did not choose me, but I chose you and appointed you so that you might go and bear fruit - fruit that will last.'

1 John 3:1 says 'How great is the love the Father has lavished on us, that we should be called children of God! And that is what we are!'

Romans 15:7 says we have been accepted by Christ.

In Jeremiah 31:1 God says 'I have loved you with an everlasting love; I have drawn you with loving-kindness.'

---

205 https://www.engageworship.org/ideas/ep-2

Ephesians 1:4 says that we are chosen in Christ before the creation of the world to be holy and blameless in God's sight.

Romans 8 says that nothing can separate you from the love that God has for you.

CLOSING REFLECTION

At the end of this book, we wanted to give you a chance to reflect on your own journey as a worship leader and worship team member, in the light of the themes we have covered.

Take some time to think about the four different characteristics of Jesus. Where have you been inspired by Jesus while reading this book, and where have you been challenged?

Use the diagram below to mark how you feel you're doing in each of the themes. Make a dot in each of the four quarters - the outer circle represents being further along in the journey and the inner circle represents the beginning of the journey. Join the dots together into a shape and look at it.

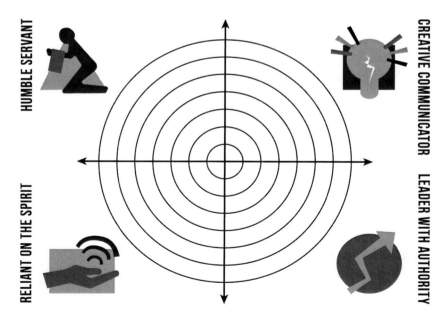

In our experience the diagonally opposite characteristics tend to pull against each other. For example strong leaders might struggle with humility, whereas natural servants can be reluctant to take authority. The shape can also reflect the season you are in - there are times when we are emphasising the creative side of worship but may not be as consciously reliant on the Spirit, or vice versa. The point of this is not to feel guilty or discouraged, but to recognise where you are in your journey right now, and how you might grow in the future. Everyone will have some areas which are stronger than others - only Jesus will have a perfectly balanced shape.

Ask God to speak to you about your shape, and reflect on the following questions:

- What can I celebrate about how God uses me in gathered worship?
- In what area would I like to grow in my worship leading, to be more like Jesus?
- What steps can I take to help this growth?
- What is one thing I can do at the next time of worship I lead, or next rehearsal I'm involved in, to put these steps into practice?
- In the areas where I'm strong, how am I helping others to grow? Can I think of one or two people that I could mentor in these areas?

You could also do the same process to reflect on the strengths and growth areas for your church worship team.

After you have reflected on these topics, hand your development in leading worship over to God by making this prayer your own:

Jesus Christ, be my leader and my
inspiration as I engage others in worship
- may I follow you and you alone.

As you humbled yourself, serving the
church even to the end, help me serve others
with your confidence and grace.

Spark my creativity and use the gifts you've given
me to communicate your truth, beauty and justice.

Come Holy Spirit, fill me up and send me out
to lead worship wherever I find myself,
to the glory of God the Father,

Amen.

BONUS: PLANNING A JOURNEY OF WORSHIP

People often ask us: 'How do you plan a worship time?'[206] There are endless different options for songs, prayers and media for worship, and it can be a challenge to know what fits where. Services can take many different shapes and formats, so our aim is not to push any specific style or structure on you. Whatever your services look like, we believe that they can be at their best when planned and led as a flowing and logical journey.

1) FINDING OUT THE INFO

Our first step is to find out all the information you can about the service. The primary things to know are the format of the service and any Bible readings and themes. Here's an example service structure that is fairly typical of what you might find in many churches:

STRUCTURE	FUNCTION	MEDIA
Welcome		
Song / Hymn		
Children's talk		
Sung Worship (15 mins)		

---

206 We also talk through this process in video 2B of the training course.

STRUCTURE	FUNCTION	MEDIA
Bible Reading (Jeremiah 29:7)		
Sermon: 'Pray for the Land of Your Exile'		
Response time		
Blessing / Final song		

Some services will be more complex, including elements like confession, creed, testimony or the Lord's Prayer. Others are far freer, perhaps composed of blocks of singing, teaching and a response. The important thing is to know the shape you are being asked to work with, and create a journey within it. It can also be useful to know:

- The season of the church year
- Other special items (baptisms, missionary talk, Communion)
- The musicians and singers you have at your disposal
- The types of people you expect to be there (regular congregation and any guests, such as baptism visitors)

Find out which aspects of the service you are expected to plan, and which things will be planned by other people. If at all possible have a conversation (or at least an email exchange) with service leaders, preachers and other contributors, to make sure that you are working together rather than in isolation from one another. Talk together about your shared aims for the service, and how the different aspects can flow together.

Read through the Bible passages for the service and any theme material provided by the preacher. Not every song or aspect of the service has to directly reflect the theme - some parts of the journey may stand alone. But it is important to be aware of the Bible and teaching content, and somehow reflect and respond to it appropriately.

2) LISTENING TO GOD

The next stage is to stop, pray and listen. We find it really helpful to pause our own thought processes and give God space to speak into our planning. If the idea of listening to God is not something you are very familiar with, we talk about it in Chapter 6.

Ask God what he wants to achieve in this coming worship time. Where should you be heading towards - receiving his empowering? Confession and forgiveness? Prayer for the nation? Response to a challenge? Listen for a sense of his heart for your community in this specific meeting.

As well as this, you may find words, scriptures, pictures, songs or worship ideas come into your mind. Whatever you sense, test it by the truth of the Bible, ideally discussing it with someone who is planning the service with you. And test your thoughts against the theme and service order. For example, if you think that worship should be an open-ended praise-party this week, does that fit in with the ten minutes you have actually been given, between the notices and the Boys' Brigade presentation?

3) PLANNING YOUR JOURNEY

You may now have a sense of direction and some ideas, but hold off planning your songs and other 'media' for one more stage of this process. This is the moment when we sketch out the shape or journey of the worship time using 'function' language. We wrote in Chapter 4 about the different 'functions' we see in the Psalms - gathering, praise, confession, intercession, adoration, response... and so on. If you write down the kind of journey you want to go on, using this language, you have a much clearer idea of where you are going in the service. For our example service we could add the following journey:

STRUCTURE	FUNCTION	MEDIA
Welcome		
Song / Hymn	Gathering / Call-to-worship	
Children's talk	Teaching: The Power of Prayer	
Sung Worship (15 mins)	Themed on God's power, leading into theme of God's love for everyone.	
Bible Reading (Jeremiah 29:7)		

STRUCTURE	FUNCTION	MEDIA
Sermon: 'Pray for the Land of Your Exile'		
Response time	Personal reflection, into prayer for our town.	
Blessing / Final song	Sending out to serve God in our town.	

4) ADDING YOUR MEDIA

Once you have this kind of structure, now is the moment to decide which songs or other media best achieve your functions. Consider music and creative elements which will fit, given the resources you have and the kind of people you have in the congregation. What you write in the 'media' column will very much depend on the kind of songs familiar to you and your congregation, the age ranges, the spiritual styles and personality types you are serving.

For our example service we are imagining a mixed congregation including both young and old, and we are pursuing a breadth of song choices to meet these varied personalities. So our Call-to-worship song is a traditional hymn, which contrasts with the fun, modern song about God's power ('Great Big God') and a simple repeated chorus everyone can join in with ('Awesome God'). 'Higher Than The Mountains' highlights God's love in a personal way, with a modern style.

STRUCTURE	FUNCTION	MEDIA
Welcome		
Song / Hymn	Gathering / Call-to-worship	'To God be the Glory'[207]
Children's talk	Teaching: The Power of Prayer	Pester Power Parable[208]
Sung Worship (15 mins)	Themed on God's power, leading into theme of God's love for everyone.	'Great Big God'[209] 'Awesome God'[210] 'Higher than the Mountains'[211]
Bible Reading (Jeremiah 29:7)		
Sermon: 'Pray for the Land of Your Exile'		
Response time	Personal reflection, into prayer for our town.	Silence, then images for prayer. Songs: 'O Lord Hear My Prayer'[212] into 'Longing for Light'[213]
Blessing / Final song	Sending out to serve God in our town.	'Build Your Kingdom'[214] or 'We are Called to be God's People'[215]

207 By Fanny Crosby, https://engageworship.org/HWJlinks
208 By Bob Hartman, https://www.engageworship.org/pester
209 By Nigel and Jo Hemming, https://engageworship.org/HWJlinks
210 Chorus of the song by Rich Mullins, https://engageworship.org/HWJlinks
211 By Brian Johnson, Christa Black Gifford, Jeremy Riddle, https://engageworship.org/HWJlinks
212 Jacques Berthier, https://engageworship.org/HWJlinks
213 https://engageworship.org/HWJlinks
214 By Rend Collective, https://engageworship.org/HWJlinks
215 By Thomas Jackson, https://engageworship.org/HWJlinks

At the end of the service we combine a simple Taizé chant ('O Lord Hear My Prayer') with a longer hymn by Bernadette Farrell ('Longing for Light'). In keeping with our suggestions about preparing for spontaneity in Chapter 6, we have prepared two possible closing songs. Depending on the mood at the time 'Build Your Kingdom' can be played in an upbeat, celebratory way or at a slower, more reflective pace. 'We are Called to be God's People' is a slower, steadier hymn we sing to a familiar tune ('Here is Love'), which would fit for a more formal sending.

Beyond music, we have also planned a fun, creative Bible reading to engage all ages (Pester Power Parable), a time of silence, and a visual way of praying involving images on a screen. These connect with different senses, learning styles and age groups. These aspects of the service may or may not be in your remit to choose, but we have included them to demonstrate a variety of ways you can engage with God.

While this will look different in your context, we would still encourage you to try out the process described above and see how it brings shape and flow to your times of gathered worship.